MW00381106

Biscuits & Scones

Southern Recipe Collection!

S. L. Watson

Copyright © 2016 S. L. Watson

All rights reserved.

ISBN: 9781549932458

All rights reserved. No part of this book may be reproduced or utilized in any form or by any means, electronic or mechanical, including photocopying and recording without express written permission from the author and/or copyright holder. This book is for informational or entertainment purposes only. Cover design S. L. Watson 2016. Picture courtesy of Canva.

The author has made every effort to ensure the information provided in this book is correct. Failure to follow directions could result in a failed recipe. The author does not assume and hereby disclaim any liability to any party for any loss, damage, illness or disruption caused by errors and omissions, whether such errors and omissions result from negligence, accident or any other cause.

The author has made every effort to provide accurate information in the creation of this book. The author accepts no responsibility and gives no warranty for any damages or loss of any kind that might be incurred by the reader or user due to actions resulting from the use of the information in this book. The user assumes complete responsibility for the use of the information in this book.

DEDICATION

To our southern heritage that made delicious biscuits what they are today!

CONTENTS

Introduction

Being from the rural South, I have made thousands of biscuits in my lifetime. My family devours biscuits whether they are sweet or savory. With over 100 recipes included in this cookbook, I am sure you will find a savory or sweet biscuit recipe to suit any occasion. Serve the biscuits with breakfast, lunch or dinner. They are great with most any meal and delicious with soups, stews, casseroles, omelets and chilis.

Now you have every biscuit recipe in my southern heritage in this great southern biscuit and scone collection.

Biscuit Making Tips

Do not handle biscuit dough anymore than necessary. Over working or handling the dough will make for tough biscuits. Place biscuits with the sides touching to make the biscuits rise higher. When cutting biscuits, do not twist the biscuit cutter. Push the cutter straight down. This will prevent the outside of your biscuits from being tough and uneven.

There are three golden rules when making biscuits. For biscuits to rise properly, you need a preheated hot oven. For best results, chill your butter, shortening or lard before using in the recipes. If your butter or lard are at room temperature, put them in the freezer for 5 minutes. Do not handle the dough more than necessary and use a light touch when folding the biscuit dough.

Whole milk will produce a soft and fluffy biscuit. You can use 2% milk but the biscuit will not be as tender. Skim or fat free milk will make a tough biscuit.

Most biscuit recipes call for whole milk. You can substitute buttermilk but I personally do not like the taste of buttermilk. I use whole milk for baking. We drink 2% milk, so I buy whole milk by the quart. I separate the whole milk into one cup containers and keep them in the freezer. You can thaw the milk quickly by setting the container in hot water for a few minutes or placing the container in the refrigerator to thaw overnight. There are many Tetra type packs of whole milk readily available at the grocery store. I buy these and keep them in the pantry so I always have whole milk on hand.

For biscuits or any baking, use a quality flour. I have used cheaper store flours and have not been satisfied with the results. I use White Lily, Gold Medal, Pillsbury or Martha White flours. If you are having trouble making fluffy biscuits, your flour may be the problem. I use White Lily for all breads and biscuits. White Lily is a regional flour but if you can order it online, it is definitely worth the purchase.

Do not use a shiny baking pan for biscuits. A cast iron skillet makes the best biscuits. If you have an old cookie sheet that has darkened in color, this is also great for biscuits. Shiny or glass pans do not produce the browning or crisp crust needed on biscuits.

1 SAVORY BISCUITS

My family loves all types of biscuits. I find myself making savory biscuits more than sweet biscuits. Savory biscuits and scones go so well with soups, stews, chilis, casseroles or virtually any meal.

Savory Drop Biscuits

Makes 1 dozen

1 3/4 cups all purpose flour
1 tbs. baking powder
1/2 tsp. salt
1/2 tsp. rubbed sage
1/2 tsp. caraway seeds
1/4 tsp. dry mustard
1 cup whole milk
1/4 cup melted unsalted butter
1 tbs. softened unsalted butter

Preheat the oven to 450°. Grease your baking sheet with 1 tablespoon softened butter. In a mixing bowl, add the all purpose flour, baking powder, salt, sage, caraway seeds and dry mustard. Stir until well blended.

Add the milk and 1/4 cup melted butter to the dry ingredients. Stir until well combined and a soft dough forms. Drop the dough by rounded tablespoonfuls onto your prepared baking sheet. With floured hands, lightly form the biscuits into a round shape. Bake for 10-12 minutes or until the biscuits are lightly browned. Remove the biscuits from the oven and serve hot.

Hearty Cheddar Biscuits

Makes about 2 dozen

2 cups all purpose flour
1 tbs. baking powder
1 tsp. salt
1/4 cup unsalted butter, chilled
1 1/2 cups shredded cheddar cheese
1/2 cup chopped onion
2 tbs. red pimento, chopped
1/4 - 1/2 cup whole milk

Preheat the oven to 425°. In a mixing bowl, add the all purpose flour, baking powder and salt. Stir until well combined. Add the butter to the dry ingredients. Using a pastry blender, cut the butter into the dry ingredients until you have coarse crumbs. You should still be able to see tiny bits of the butter when done.

Add the cheddar cheese, onion and pimento to the bowl. Add 1/4 cup milk and mix until a soft dough forms. Add the remaining milk to the bowl if needed to make a moist but soft dough.

Lightly flour your work surface. Place the dough on the work surface. Lightly knead the dough 10 times. Roll the dough out to 1/2" thickness. Using a 2" biscuit cutter, cut out the biscuits. Cut the biscuits close together to cut out as many as possible on the first cutting. Roll out the dough scraps and cut out the remaining biscuits. Place the biscuits on an ungreased baking sheet. Bake for 12-15 minutes or until the biscuits are golden brown.

Tomato Biscuits

Makes about 2 dozen

2 cups all purpose flour
1 tbs. plus 1 tsp. baking powder
1 tsp. granulated sugar
1/2 tsp. salt
1/4 tsp. baking soda
Pinch of ground ginger
1/4 cup plus 1 tbs. cold vegetable shortening
1 cup shredded sharp cheddar cheese
1 cup cold tomato juice

Preheat the oven to 400°. Grease a baking sheet with 1 tablespoon vegetable shortening. In a mixing bowl, add the all purpose flour, baking powder, granulated sugar, salt, baking soda and ginger. Stir until well combined. Add 1/4 cup vegetable shortening to the dry ingredients. Using a pastry blender, cut the shortening into the dry ingredients until you have coarse crumbs. Add the cheddar cheese and tomato juice. Stir only until the dough is moistened and combined.

Lightly flour your work surface. Place the dough on the work surface. With the palm of your hand, slightly flatten the dough. Fold the dough over and slightly flatten the dough again. Turn the dough about 1/4 turn and fold the dough over again. Repeat two more times. The dough should be smooth and soft.

Pat the dough to a 1/2" thickness with your hands. Using a 1 1/2" biscuit cutter, cut out the biscuits. Lightly pat out the dough scraps again to cut out the remaining biscuits. Place the biscuits on your baking sheet. Bake for 10-12 minutes or until the biscuits are done and lightly browned. Remove the biscuits from the oven and serve.

Tomato Herb Biscuits

Makes 10 biscuits

1/3 cup olive oil
2 cups self rising flour
3/4 cup buttermilk
1/2 cup grated Parmesan cheese
1/4 cup sun dried tomatoes in oil, minced
1 tsp. dried Italian seasoning
1/4 tsp. black pepper
2 tbs. unsalted butter, melted

Preheat the oven to 425°. In a mixing bowl, add the olive oil, self rising flour, buttermilk, Parmesan cheese, tomatoes, Italian seasoning and black pepper. Stir until well combined and a soft dough forms.

Lightly flour your work surface. Place the dough on the work surface. With the palm of your hand, slightly flatten the dough. Fold the dough over and slightly flatten the dough again. Turn the dough about 1/4 turn and fold the dough over again. Repeat two more times. The dough should be smooth and soft.

Pat the dough to a 1/2" thickness with your hands. Using a 2 1/2" biscuit cutter, cut out the biscuits. Lightly pat out the dough scraps again to cut out the remaining biscuits. Place the biscuits on your baking sheet. Bake for 10-12 minutes or until the biscuits are done and lightly browned. Remove the biscuits from the oven and brush the melted butter over the biscuits before serving. Serve the biscuits hot.

Herb Roquefort Biscuits

Makes 12 biscuits

3 oz. pkg. Roquefort cheese, crumbled
2 tbs. minced green onion tops
1 tsp. dried basil
1/2 tsp. dried thyme
2 cups all purpose flour
1 tbs. baking powder
1/2 tsp. salt
1/4 tsp. baking soda
1/4 cup plus 2 tbs. unsalted butter, chilled
3/4 cup whole milk
1 tsp. vegetable shortening

Cut the butter into small pieces. Grease a baking sheet with the vegetable shortening. Preheat the oven to 450°.

In a small bowl, add the Roquefort cheese, green onion, basil and thyme. Stir until well combined. The mixture will be crumbly. In a separate bowl, add the all purpose flour, baking powder, salt and baking soda. Stir until combined.

Add the Roquefort cheese blend and the butter to the dry ingredients. Using a pastry blender, cut the butter and cheese into the dry ingredients until you have coarse crumbs. Add the milk and stir only until the dough is moistened and combined.

Lightly flour your work surface. Place the dough on the surface. With the palm of your hand, slightly flatten the dough. Fold the dough over and slightly flatten the dough again. Turn the dough about 1/4 turn and fold the dough over again. Repeat two more times. The dough should be smooth and soft.

Pat the dough to a 1/2" thickness with your hands. Using a 2 1/2" biscuit cutter, cut out the biscuits. Lightly pat out the dough scraps again to cut out the remaining biscuits. Place the biscuits on your baking sheet. Bake for 13-15 minutes or until the biscuits are done and lightly browned. Remove the biscuits from the oven and serve.

Pesto Pecan Biscuits

Makes about 16 biscuits

1 envelope rapid rise yeast
1 tbs. granulated sugar
3/4 cup warm water
4 cups Bisquick
1/2 cup diced pecans
1 cup whole milk
1/4 cup melted unsalted butter
2 tbs. prepared pesto
16 pecan halves

In a mixing bowl, add the yeast, granulated sugar and warm water. Stir until the yeast dissolves and let the yeast sit for 5 minutes. Add the Bisquick, diced pecans, milk, butter and pesto to the bowl. Stir only until the dough is moistened and well combined.

Lightly flour your work surface. Place the dough on the work surface. With the palm of your hand, slightly flatten the dough. Fold the dough over and slightly flatten the dough again. Turn the dough about 1/4 turn and fold the dough over again. Repeat two more times. The dough should be smooth and soft.

Pat the dough to a 1" thickness with your hands. Using a 2" biscuit cutter, cut out the biscuits. Lightly pat out the dough scraps again to cut out the remaining biscuits. Place the biscuits on your baking sheet. Place a pecan half in the center of each biscuit. Bake for 20-25 minutes or until the biscuits are done and golden brown. Remove the biscuits from the oven and serve.

Cheesy Onion Biscuits

Makes 8 biscuits

2 cups all purpose flour
3 tbs. instant nonfat dry milk powder
4 tsp. baking powder
1/3 cup chilled unsalted butter
1/2 cup grated Parmesan cheese
2 tbs. finely chopped green onions
3/4 cup water
1 tbs. vegetable shortening

Preheat the oven to 400°. Grease your baking sheet with the vegetable shortening. In a mixing bowl, add the all purpose flour, dry milk powder, baking powder and butter. Using a pastry blender, cut the butter into the dry ingredients until you have coarse crumbs. Stir in the Parmesan cheese and green onions. Add the water to the dry ingredients and stir only until the dough is moistened and combined.

Lightly flour your work surface. Place the dough on the work surface. With the palm of your hand, slightly flatten the dough. Fold the dough over and slightly flatten the dough again. Turn the dough about 1/4 turn and fold the dough over again. Repeat three more times. The dough should be smooth and soft.

Pat the dough to a 1/2" thickness with your hands. Using a 3" biscuit cutter, cut out the biscuits. Lightly pat out the dough scraps again to cut out the remaining biscuits. Place the biscuits on your baking sheet. Bake for 15 minutes or until the biscuits are done and golden brown. Remove the biscuits from the oven and serve.

Herb Biscuits

Makes 12 biscuits

2 cups all purpose flour
1 tbs. baking powder
1/2 tsp. baking soda
1/4 tsp. salt
1/4 tsp. dried thyme
1/4 tsp. dried rosemary
1/4 tsp. dried basil
1/4 cup unsalted butter, chilled
3/4 cup whole milk
1 tbs. vegetable shortening

Preheat the oven to 400°. Grease your baking sheet with the vegetable shortening . In a mixing bowl, add the all purpose flour, baking powder, baking soda, salt, thyme, rosemary, basil and butter. Using a pastry blender, cut the butter into the dry ingredients until you have coarse crumbs. Add the milk to the dry ingredients and stir only until the dough is moistened and combined.

Lightly flour your work surface. Place the dough on the work surface. With the palm of your hand, slightly flatten the dough. Fold the dough over and slightly flatten the dough again. Turn the dough about 1/4 turn and fold the dough over again. Repeat two more times. The dough should be smooth and soft.

Pat the dough to a 1/2" thickness with your hands. Using a 2 1/2" biscuit cutter, cut out the biscuits. Lightly pat out the dough scraps again to cut out the remaining biscuits. Place the biscuits on your baking sheet. Bake for 10-12 minutes or until the biscuits are done and golden brown. Remove the biscuits from the oven and serve.

Raised Biscuits with Ham

Makes 3 dozen

1 envelope active dry yeast
1/2 cup warm water
2 cups whole milk
5 1/2 cups all purpose flour
1 1/2 tbs. baking powder
1 1/2 tsp. salt
1/2 tsp. baking soda
1/4 cup granulated sugar
3/4 cup vegetable shortening
8 oz. shaved country ham
1 tbs. vegetable shortening

In a small bowl, add the yeast and warm water. Stir until the yeast dissolves and let the yeast sit for 5 minutes. Stir the milk into the yeast mixture. In a mixing bowl, add the all purpose flour, baking powder, salt, baking soda and granulated sugar. Stir until well combined. Add 3/4 cup vegetable shortening to the dry ingredients. Using a pastry blender, cut the shortening into the dry ingredients until you have coarse crumbs. Add the yeast mixture to the dry ingredients. Using a fork, mix until the dough is moistened.

Lightly flour your work surface. Turn the dough onto your work surface and knead the dough 5 times. Roll the dough out to 1/2" thickness. Using a 2" biscuit cutter, cut out the biscuits. Roll out the dough scraps again and cut out the remaining biscuits. Grease a large baking sheet with 1 tablespoon vegetable shortening. Place the biscuits on the baking sheet.

Cover the biscuits with a clean dish towel and place the pan in a warm place to rise. The biscuits need to rise for 1 hour.

Preheat the oven to 425°. Bake for 10-12 minutes or until the biscuits are done and golden brown. Remove the biscuits from the oven and fill with the country ham. Serve hot.

Bacon Cheese Biscuits

Makes about 16 biscuits

2 cups self rising flour
1 tbs. granulated sugar
1/2 tsp. baking soda
1/3 cup cold vegetable shortening
1 cup whole milk
1 1/2 cups crumbled cooked bacon
1 cup shredded cheddar cheese
1 tbs. vegetable shortening

Preheat the oven to 425°. Grease your baking sheet with 1 tablespoon vegetable shortening. In a mixing bowl, add the self rising flour, granulated sugar, baking soda and 1/3 cup vegetable shortening. Using a pastry blender, cut the shortening into the dry ingredients until you have coarse crumbs.

Add the milk, cheese and bacon to the bowl. Stir only until the dough is moistened and combined. Depending upon the dryness of the cheese and bacon, you may need to add a tablespoon or two additional milk to the dough. You need a moist but soft dough.

Lightly flour your work surface. Place the dough on the work surface. With the palm of your hand, slightly flatten the dough. Fold the dough over and slightly flatten the dough again. Turn the dough about 1/4 turn and fold the dough over again. Repeat two more times. The dough should be smooth and soft.

Pat the dough to a 1/2" thickness with your hands. Using a 2" biscuit cutter, cut out the biscuits. Lightly pat out the dough scraps again to cut out the remaining biscuits. Place the biscuits on your baking sheet. Bake for 10-12 minutes or until the biscuits are done and lightly browned. Remove the biscuits from the oven and serve.

Potato Bacon Biscuits

Makes 10 biscuits

1 cup self rising flour
1 cup instant potato flakes
8 slices bacon, cooked and crumbled
1/2 cup shredded cheddar cheese
1/3 cup unsalted butter, chilled
3/4 cup whole milk
2 tbs. melted unsalted butter

Preheat the oven to 425°. In a mixing bowl, add the self rising flour, potato flakes and 1/3 cup butter. Using a pastry blender, cut the butter into the dry ingredients until you have coarse crumbs. Stir in the cheddar cheese and bacon. Add the milk to the dry ingredients and stir only until the dough is moistened and combined.

Lightly flour your work surface. Place the dough on the work surface. With the palm of your hand, slightly flatten the dough. Fold the dough over and slightly flatten the dough again. Turn the dough about 1/4 turn and fold the dough over again. Repeat two more times. The dough should be smooth and soft.

Pat the dough to a 3/4" thickness with your hands. Using a 2 1/2" biscuit cutter, cut out the biscuits. Lightly pat out the dough scraps again to cut out the remaining biscuits. Place the biscuits on an ungreased baking sheet. Brush the biscuits with the melted butter. Bake for 12-14 minutes or until the biscuits are done and golden brown. Remove the biscuits from the oven and serve.

Cheese and Chive Biscuits

Makes 12 biscuits

2 cups all purpose flour
1 tbs. baking powder
3/4 tsp. salt
1/4 cup chilled unsalted butter
1/2 cup shredded sharp cheddar cheese
1/4 cup chopped fresh chives
1 cup whole milk
1 tbs. unsalted butter, melted
2 tsp. water

Preheat the oven to 450°. In a mixing bowl, add the all purpose flour, baking powder, salt and 1/4 cup butter. Using a pastry blender, cut the butter into the dry ingredients until you have coarse crumbs. Stir in the cheddar cheese and chives. Add the milk to the dry ingredients and stir only until the dough is moistened and combined.

Lightly flour your work surface. Place the dough on the work surface. With the palm of your hand, slightly flatten the dough. Fold the dough over and slightly flatten the dough again. Turn the dough about 1/4 turn and fold the dough over again. Repeat two more times. The dough should be smooth and soft.

Pat the dough to a 3/4" thickness with your hands. Using a 2 1/2" biscuit cutter, cut out the biscuits. Lightly pat out the dough scraps again to cut out the remaining biscuits. Place the biscuits on an ungreased baking sheet. In a small bowl, stir together the melted butter and water. Brush the mixture over the top of the biscuits. Bake for 10-12 minutes or until the biscuits are done and golden brown. Remove the biscuits from the oven and serve.

Cornmeal Jalapeño Biscuits

Makes 10 biscuits

1/3 cup chilled unsalted butter
1 cup self rising flour
1 cup self rising white or yellow cornmeal
1 cup shredded Pepper Jack cheese
1 jalapeño pepper, minced
3/4 cup whole milk
2 tbs. melted unsalted butter

Preheat the oven to 425°. In a mixing bowl, add the self rising flour, cornmeal and 1/3 cup butter. Using a pastry blender, cut the butter into the dry ingredients until you have coarse crumbs. Stir in the Pepper Jack cheese and jalapeño pepper. Add the milk to the dry ingredients and stir only until the dough is moistened and combined.

Lightly flour your work surface. Place the dough on the work surface. With the palm of your hand, slightly flatten the dough. Fold the dough over and slightly flatten the dough again. Turn the dough about 1/4 turn and fold the dough over again. Repeat two more times. The dough should be smooth and soft.

Pat the dough to a 3/4" thickness with your hands. Using a 2 1/2" biscuit cutter, cut out the biscuits. Lightly pat out the dough again to cut out the remaining biscuits. Place the biscuits on an ungreased baking sheet. Brush the biscuits with the melted butter. Bake for 12-14 minutes or until the biscuits are done and golden brown. Remove the biscuits from the oven and serve.

Jalapeño Biscuits

Makes about 18 biscuits

4 cups all purpose flour
2 tbs. baking powder
1 tsp. salt
2/3 cup unsalted butter, chilled
1/4 cup minced jalapeño peppers
1 1/2 cups whole milk
2 tbs. melted unsalted butter
1 tbs. vegetable shortening

Preheat the oven to 425°. Grease a large baking sheet with the vegetable shortening. Cut the chilled butter into small pieces. In a mixing bowl, add the all purpose flour, baking powder, salt and 2/3 cup butter. Using a pastry blender, cut the butter into the dry ingredients until you have coarse crumbs. Stir in the jalapeño pepper. Add the milk to the dry ingredients and stir only until the dough is moistened and combined. You may need to add a tablespoon or two additional milk to make a soft dough.

Lightly flour your work surface. Place the dough on the work surface. With the palm of your hand, slightly flatten the dough. Fold the dough over and slightly flatten the dough again. Turn the dough about 1/4 turn and fold the dough over again. Repeat two more times. The dough should be smooth and soft.

Pat the dough to a 3/4" thickness with your hands. Using a 2 1/2" biscuit cutter, cut out the biscuits. Lightly pat out the dough scraps again to cut out the remaining biscuits. Place the biscuits on your baking sheet. Brush the melted butter over the biscuits. Bake for 12-14 minutes or until the biscuits are done and golden brown. Remove the biscuits from the oven and serve.

Basil Biscuits

Makes 1 dozen

1 pkg. active dry yeast
2 tbs. warm water
1 cup whole milk
2 1/2 cups all purpose flour
1 1/2 tsp. baking powder
1/2 tsp. baking soda
1/4 tsp. salt
2 tbs. granulated sugar
1/2 cup plus 1 tbs. vegetable shortening
1/4 cup finely chopped fresh basil
2 tbs. finely chopped oil packed sun dried tomatoes

In a mixing bowl, add the yeast and warm water. Stir until the yeast dissolves and let the yeast sit for 5 minutes. Stir the milk into the yeast mixture and set the bowl aside.

In a mixing bowl, add the all purpose flour, baking powder, baking soda, salt and granulated sugar. Add 1/2 cup shortening to the dry ingredients. Using a pastry blender, cut the shortening into the dry ingredients until you have coarse crumbs.

Add the yeast mixture, basil and tomatoes to the dry ingredients. Stir only until combined. The dough will be loose and sticky.

Heavily flour your work surface. Toss the dough in the flour until the dough is well coated with the flour. Place the dough on the work surface. With the palm of your hand, slightly flatten the dough. Fold the dough over and slightly flatten the dough again. Turn the dough about 1/4 turn and fold the dough over again. Repeat three more times. The dough should smooth and soft.

Pat the dough to a 1/2" thickness with your hands. Using a 2 1/2" biscuit cutter, cut out the biscuits. Lightly pat out the dough scraps again to cut out the remaining biscuits. Grease your baking sheet with 1 tablespoon vegetable shortening. Place the biscuits on your baking sheet.

Cover the biscuits with a clean dish towel and let the biscuits rise in a warm place for 30 minutes. Preheat the oven to 450°. Bake for 10-12 minutes or until the biscuits are done and golden brown. Serve the biscuits hot.

Taco Spiced Cornmeal Biscuits

Makes 12 biscuits

1 3/4 cups all purpose flour
1/3 cup plain white cornmeal
2 1/2 tsp. baking powder
1/2 tsp. baking soda
3/4 tsp. salt
1 1/2 tbs. granulated sugar
2 tsp. taco seasoning mix
6 tbs. cold unsalted butter
3/4 to 1 cup buttermilk
1 tbs. vegetable shortening

Preheat the oven to 425°. Grease your baking pan with the vegetable shortening. In a mixing bowl, add the all purpose flour, cornmeal, baking powder, baking soda, salt, granulated sugar and taco seasoning mix. Stir until well combined.

Add the butter to the dry ingredients. Using a pastry blender, cut the butter into the dry ingredients until you have coarse crumbs. You should still be able to see tiny pieces of butter when finished. Add 3/4 cup buttermilk and stir only until the dough is moistened. The dough will leave the sides of the bowl when ready. Add the remaining milk if needed to make a soft and moist dough.

Lightly flour your work surface. Place the dough on the work surface and knead the dough a couple times. Do not over work the dough or the biscuits will be tough. Pat the dough out to a 3/4" thickness.

Using a 2" round biscuit cutter, cut out the biscuits. Roll out the remaining scraps of dough and cut out the remaining biscuits. Place the biscuits on the greased baking sheet with the sides touching each other. Bake for 12-15 minutes or until the biscuits are golden brown.

Brush butter across the biscuits if desired. You can substitute any herb combination for the taco seasoning if desired.

Pimento Cheese Biscuits

You can substitute 2 cups store bought pimento cheese if desired but homemade pimento cheese is so much better. Makes 12 biscuits.

2 cups shredded cheddar cheese
2 oz. jar red diced pimentos, drained well
1/3 cup mayonnaise
1/4 tsp. dry mustard
1/8 tsp. cayenne pepper
2 cups self rising flour
3/4 cup whole milk
1/4 cup vegetable shortening, cold
1 tbs. vegetable shortening

In a mixing bowl, add the cheddar cheese, pimentos, mayonnaise, dry mustard and cayenne pepper. Stir until well combined. Set the pimento cheese aside for now.

Preheat the oven to 450°. Grease your baking pan with 1 tablespoon vegetable shortening. In a mixing bowl, add the self rising flour and 1/4 cup vegetable shortening. Using a pastry blender, cut the shortening into the flour until you have coarse crumbs. You should still be able to see tiny pieces of shortening when done. Add the milk and stir only until the dough is moistened and begins to leave the sides of the bowl.

Lightly flour your work surface. Place the dough on the work surface. Do not add additional flour unless needed to make a soft dough that holds together. Flatten the dough with your hand. Fold the dough in half and flatten the dough again. Pat the dough into a 14 x 10 inch rectangle. Spread the pimento cheese over the dough.

Starting with a long end, roll the dough up like a jelly roll. Roll the dough tightly but not so tight as to damage the dough. Using a sharp knife, cut the dough into slices about 3/4" thick. Place the biscuits on your prepared pan with the sides touching each other. Bake for 13-16 minutes or until the biscuits are golden brown.

Hearty Meat & Cheese Pan Biscuits

Makes 6 servings

1 tbs. butter
2 1/4 cups Bisquick
3/4 cup whole milk
4 oz. cooked & crumbled pork sausage
4 slices bacon, cooked & crumbled
1/2 cup shredded cheddar cheese
1/2 cup shredded Mozzarella cheese

Preheat the oven to 450°. Place the butter in a 9" square baking pan and place the pan in the oven until the butter melts. In a mixing bowl, add the Bisquick and milk. Stir until a soft dough forms. Stir in the sausage, bacon, cheddar cheese and the mozzarella cheese. Remove the hot pan from the oven and place the dough into the pan. Spread the dough over the melted butter. Use your hands to smooth the dough if needed.

Be careful! The pan will be very hot. Bake for 10-15 minutes or until the biscuits are done and golden brown. Cut into squares and serve.

Blue Cheese & Olive Drop Biscuits

Makes about 16-20 small drop biscuits

2 cups self rising flour
1/4 tsp. cayenne pepper
1/4 cup vegetable shortening, chilled
1 cup crumbled blue cheese
1/4 cup Kalamata olives, diced
1 tsp. fresh thyme, minced
3/4 cup whole milk
1 tbs. vegetable shortening
2 tbs. unsalted butter, melted

Preheat the oven to 425°. Grease your baking sheet with 1 tablespoon vegetable shortening. In a mixing bowl, add the self rising flour, cayenne pepper and 1/4 cup vegetable shortening. Using a pastry blender, cut the shortening into the flour until you have coarse crumbs. You should still be able to see tiny pieces of shortening when done.

Add the blue cheese, olives, thyme and milk to the bowl. Stir only until the dough is moistened and combined. Drop the dough by tablespoonfuls on the prepared baking sheet. Space the biscuits about 2" apart. Bake for 12-15 minutes or until the biscuits are done and golden brown. Remove the biscuits from the oven and brush the melted butter across the biscuits. Serve these biscuits for dinner in place of dinner rolls. They are excellent with soups, stews, salads or most casseroles.

Savory Cheddar Pecan Biscuits

These biscuits are perfect for appetizers, snacking, brunch and breakfast. Makes 6 dozen bite size biscuits.

2 cups shredded sharp cheddar cheese
2 1/4 cups all purpose flour
1 cup unsalted butter, softened
1 cup chopped pecans
1 tsp. Worcestershire sauce
1/2 tsp. salt
1/2 tsp. cayenne pepper
3/4 to 1 cup whole milk

Preheat the oven to 425°. Spray your baking sheets with non stick cooking spray. Spray the sheets well or these biscuits will stick. Add all the ingredients to a mixing bowl. Stir until well combined and a moist dough forms. The dough should leave the sides of the bowl when ready. Stir quickly and do not over work the dough or the biscuits will be tough. Depending upon the flour and cheese used, you may need to add a tablespoon or two additional milk to the dough.

Drop the biscuits by teaspoonfuls onto the baking sheets. Space the biscuits about 2" apart on the baking sheets. Bake for 12 minutes or until the biscuits are golden brown. Remove the biscuits from the oven and serve hot.

Cayenne Cheddar Biscuits

Makes 3 dozen

2 cups all purpose flour
2 tsp. baking powder
1/2 tsp. salt
3/4 tsp. cayenne pepper
1/4 cup plus 2 tbs. vegetable shortening
1 cup shredded sharp cheddar cheese
1 cup whole milk

Preheat the oven to 450°. Grease your baking sheets with 2 tablespoons vegetable shortening. In a mixing bowl, add the all purpose flour, baking powder, cayenne pepper and salt. Stir until well combined. Add 1/4 cup vegetable shortening and cheddar cheese to the dry ingredients. Using a pastry blender, cut the shortening and cheddar cheese into the dry ingredients until you have coarse crumbs.

Add the milk to the dry ingredients. Stir only until the dough is moistened and the dough begins to leave the sides of the bowl. Drop the biscuits by teaspoonfuls onto the baking sheets. Space the biscuits about 2" apart on the baking sheets. Bake for 12 minutes or until the biscuits are done and golden brown. Remove the biscuits from the oven and serve hot with your favorite butter.

Sesame Cheddar Appetizer Biscuits

Makes about 30 biscuits

1 1/2 cups all purpose flour
1 cup shredded sharp cheddar cheese
1/2 tsp. cayenne pepper
3 tbs. sesame seeds
1/2 cup unsalted butter, softened
1 egg, beaten
1/4 tsp. water
2 tbs. vegetable shortening

Preheat the oven to 400°. Grease your baking sheets with the vegetable shortening. In a mixing bowl, add the all purpose flour, cheddar cheese, cayenne pepper and sesame seeds. Stir until well combined. Add the butter to the dry ingredients. Using a pastry blender, cut the butter into the dry ingredients until you have coarse crumbs.

Add the egg and water to the dry ingredients. Using your hands, mix until the dough is moistened and combined. Shape the dough into 1" balls. Place the biscuits on your baking sheets spacing them about 1" apart. Bake for 15 minutes or until the biscuits are done and golden brown. Remove the biscuits from the oven and serve with melted butter or your favorite dipping sauces.

Bacon, Cheddar and Tomato Biscuit Sandwiches

This is an old Southern favorite for breakfast or lunch. This biscuit is made often when the tomatoes are ripe from the garden. Makes about 15-16 biscuits.

3 cups self rising flour
6 tbs. unsalted butter, chilled
2 cups shredded cheddar cheese
10 slices bacon, cooked and crumbled
1 1/3 cups whole milk
Mayonnaise
18 slices ripe red tomato
1 tbs. vegetable shortening
2 tbs. unsalted butter, melted

Preheat the oven to 425°. Grease your baking sheet with the vegetable shortening. In a mixing bowl, add the self rising flour and 6 tablespoons butter. Using a pastry blender, cut the butter into the flour until you have coarse crumbs. You should still see tiny pieces of butter when finished.

Add the cheddar cheese, bacon and milk to the bowl. Stir until the dough is combined and moistened. Depending upon the dryness of the cheese, you may need to add another tablespoon or two of milk. The dough should be moist.

Using a 1/4 cup measure, drop the dough by 1/4 cupfuls onto the baking sheet. Each biscuit should have about a 1/4 cupful of dough. Don't level the dough off in the cup. An estimated amount is fine to use. Pat the biscuits down slightly with lightly floured hands if desired.

Bake for 12-15 minutes or until the biscuits are done and golden brown. Remove the biscuits from the oven and brush with the melted butter. Split each biscuit open and spread with mayonnaise to your taste. Place a slice of tomato on one biscuit half. Top with the remaining biscuit half and enjoy.

Taco Drop Biscuits

Makes 18-22 drop biscuits

2 cups self rising flour
1/4 cup vegetable shortening
1/2 cup whole milk
1/4 cup taco sauce
1/2 cup shredded cheddar cheese
1 tsp. dried minced onion
3 tbs. unsalted butter, melted

Preheat the oven to 450°. Grease your baking sheet with 1 tablespoon melted butter. In a mixing bowl, add the self rising flour and vegetable shortening. Using a pastry blender, cut the shortening into the flour until you have coarse crumbs. You should still be able to see tiny pieces of shortening when done.

Add the milk, taco sauce, cheddar cheese and onion to the bowl. Stir until the dough is well combined. Drop the dough by tablespoonfuls onto your baking sheet. Space the biscuits about 1" apart on the baking sheet. Bake for 8-10 minutes or until the biscuits are done and browned. Remove the biscuits from the oven and brush 2 tablespoons melted butter across the tops of the biscuits.

Taco Sauce Biscuit Bites

Makes 18 biscuits

1/4 cup taco sauce (I use Ortega)
1/4 cup whole milk
1/2 tsp. instant dried onion
2 cups Bisquick
2 tsp. unsalted butter, melted
2 tbs. grated Parmesan cheese

Preheat the oven to 450°. Lightly spray a baking sheet with non stick cooking spray. In a mixing bowl, add the taco sauce, milk and onion. Stir until well combined and let the mixture sit for 5 minutes. Add the Bisquick and stir only until the dough is moistened and combined.

Lightly flour your work surface. Place the dough on your surface. Roll the dough to 1/2" thickness. Using a 1 1/2" biscuit cutter, cut out the biscuits. Cut the biscuits as close together as possible on the first cutting. Roll the dough scraps out again and cut out the remaining biscuits.

Place the biscuits on the baking sheet. Brush the melted butter over the tops of the biscuits. Sprinkle the Parmesan cheese over the top. Bake for 8-10 minutes or until the biscuits are golden brown. Remove the biscuits from the oven and serve hot.

Parsley Biscuits

Makes 12 biscuits

2 cups all purpose flour
1 tbs. baking powder
1/4 tsp. baking soda
3/4 tsp. salt
1 tbs. granulated sugar
1/4 cup unsalted butter
2 tbs. vegetable oil
3 tbs. fresh chopped parsley
3/4 cup whole milk
3 tbs. melted butter

Preheat the oven to 425°. Grease your baking pan with 1 tablespoon melted butter. In a mixing bowl, add the all purpose flour, baking powder, baking soda, salt, granulated sugar and 1/4 cup butter. Using a pastry blender, cut the butter into the dry ingredients. The dough should resemble coarse crumbs and you should still see tiny pieces of butter in the dough when done.

Add the parsley, milk and vegetable oil to the dough. Stir only until a dough forms or about 1 minute. Lightly flour your work surface. Place the dough on the work surface. Pat the dough out to 1/2" thickness. Fold the dough in half and then in half again, rotating the dough slightly each time you fold. Repeat this process three or four times to form layers. Pat the dough to 3/4" thickness. Cut the biscuits out using a 2" biscuit cutter. Roll the dough scraps out again and cut out the remaining biscuits. Place the biscuits on the prepared pan.

Bake for 12-15 minutes or until the biscuits are done and golden brown. Remove the biscuits from the oven and brush with 2 tablespoons melted butter.

Cream Cheese and Chive Biscuits

Makes about 12 biscuits

2 1/2 cups all purpose flour
1 tbs. baking powder
1/4 tsp. baking soda
2 tsp. granulated sugar
1 tsp. salt
4 tbs. fresh minced chives
5 tbs. cold unsalted butter
4 oz. cold cream cheese
1 cup whole milk
2 tbs. unsalted butter, melted
1 tbs. vegetable shortening

Preheat the oven to 425°. Grease your baking sheet with vegetable shortening. In a mixing bowl, add the all purpose flour, baking powder, baking soda, granulated sugar, salt and chives. Stir until well combined.

Add the cream cheese and 5 tablespoons butter. Using a pastry blender, cut the butter and cream cheese into the dry ingredients until you have coarse crumbs. Add the milk and stir only enough to moisten the dough. The dough should leave the sides of the bowl when moistened.

Lightly flour your work surface. Place the dough on the work surface. Do not add additional flour unless needed to make a soft dough that holds together. Flatten the dough with your hand. Fold the dough in half and flatten the dough again. Repeat 2 more times. Do not over work the dough or the biscuits will be tough.

Pat the dough out to a 3/4" thickness. Using a 2" biscuit cutter, cut out the biscuits and place each biscuit on the baking sheet. Roll the scraps of dough again and cut out the remaining biscuits. Bake for 13-16 minutes or until the biscuits are golden brown. Remove the biscuits from the oven and brush the melted butter across the top of the biscuits.

Beer and Cheddar Biscuits

Makes 12 biscuits

2 1/4 cups all purpose flour
1 tbs. granulated sugar
1 tbs. baking powder
1/2 tsp. salt
1/2 tsp. baking soda
6 tbs. unsalted butter, cold
1 cup shredded sharp cheddar cheese
3/4 cup plus 2 tbs. stout beer
2 tbs. unsalted butter, melted
1 tbs. vegetable shortening

Preheat the oven to 425°. Grease your baking pan with the vegetable shortening. In a mixing bowl, add the all purpose flour, granulated sugar, baking powder, salt, baking soda and cheese. Stir until well combined. Add 6 tablespoons cold butter. Using a pastry blender, cut the butter into the dough until you have coarse crumbs. Add the beer and mix only until the dough is combined and moistened.

Lightly flour your work surface. Place the dough on the work surface. Do not add additional flour unless needed to make a soft dough that holds together. Flatten the dough with your hand. Fold the dough in half and flatten the dough again. Repeat 2 more times. Do not over work the dough or the biscuits will be tough.

Pat the dough out to a 3/4" thickness. Using a 2" biscuit cutter, cut out the biscuits and place each biscuit on the baking sheet. Roll the scraps of dough again and cut out the remaining biscuits. Bake for 13-16 minutes or until the biscuits are golden brown. Remove the biscuits from the oven and brush the melted butter across the top of the biscuits.

Swiss Cheese and Beer Sage Biscuits

Makes 10 biscuits

1/3 cup unsalted butter
2 cups self rising flour
3/4 cup beer
1 cup shredded Swiss cheese
1 tsp. rubbed sage
2 tbs. unsalted butter, melted

Preheat the oven to 425°. In a mixing bowl, add 1/3 cup butter and self rising flour. Using a pastry blender, cut the butter into the flour until you have coarse crumbs. Add the beer, Swiss cheese and sage to the bowl. Stir until well combined and a soft dough forms.

Lightly flour your work surface. Place the dough on the work surface. With the palm of your hand, slightly flatten the dough. Fold the dough over and slightly flatten the dough again. Turn the dough about 1/4 turn and fold the dough over again. Repeat two more times. The dough should be smooth and soft.

Pat the dough to a 1/2" thickness with your hands. Using a 2 1/2" biscuit cutter, cut out the biscuits. Lightly pat out the dough again to cut out all the biscuits. Place the biscuits on an ungreased baking sheet. Bake for 10-12 minutes or until the biscuits are done and lightly browned. Remove the biscuits from the oven and brush 2 tablespoons melted butter over the biscuits before serving. Serve the biscuits hot.

Duck Fat Biscuits

Makes 10-12 biscuits

2 1/4 cups all purpose flour
1 tbs. plus 1 tsp. baking powder
1/4 tsp. baking soda
3//4 tsp. salt
3/4 to 1 cup buttermilk
1 tbs. vegetable shortening
2 tbs. unsalted butter, melted
4 tbs. cold duck fat

Preheat the oven to 425°. Grease your baking pan with the vegetable shortening. In a mixing bowl, add the all purpose flour, baking powder, baking soda and salt. Stir until well combined.

Using your fingers, add the duck fat and work the duck fat into the dry ingredients. You should still be able to see tiny pieces of duck fat when done. Add 3/4 cup buttermilk and stir until the dough is moistened and combined. Use the remaining buttermilk if needed to make a soft dough.

Lightly flour your work surface. Place the dough on the work surface. Do not add additional flour unless needed to make a soft dough that holds together. Flatten the dough with your hand. Fold the dough in half and flatten the dough again. Repeat 2 more times. Do not over work the dough or the biscuits will be tough.

Pat the dough out to a 3/4" thickness. Using a 2" biscuit cutter, cut out the biscuits and place each biscuit on the baking sheet. Roll the scraps of dough again and cut out the remaining biscuits. Bake for 13-16 minutes or until the biscuits are golden brown. Remove the biscuits from the oven and brush the melted butter across the top of the biscuits.

Savory Whole Wheat Biscuits

Makes about 10-12 biscuits

1 1/4 cups all purpose flour
1 cup whole wheat flour
1 tbs. baking powder
1/4 tsp. baking soda
3/4 tsp. salt
1 tbs. granulated sugar
5 tbs. unsalted butter, cold
3 green onions, chopped
2 tbs. fresh minced parsley
3/4 cup to 1 cup whole milk or buttermilk
1 tbs. vegetable shortening
2 tbs. unsalted butter, melted

Preheat the oven to 425°. Grease your baking pan with the vegetable shortening. In a mixing bowl, add the all purpose flour, whole wheat flour, baking powder, baking soda, salt, granulated sugar, green onions and parsley. Stir until well combined.

Add 5 tablespoons butter to the bowl. Using a pastry blender, cut the butter into the dry ingredients until you have coarse crumbs. Add 3/4 cup milk and mix only until the dough is moistened and combined. Add the remaining milk if needed to make a soft dough.

Lightly flour your work surface. Place the dough on the work surface. Do not add additional flour unless needed to make a soft dough that holds together. Flatten the dough with your hand. Fold the dough in half and flatten the dough again. Repeat 2 more times. Do not over work the dough or the biscuits will be tough.

Pat the dough out to a 3/4" thickness. Using a 2" biscuit cutter, cut out the biscuits and place each biscuit on the baking sheet. Roll the scraps of dough again and cut out the remaining biscuits. Bake for 13-16 minutes or until the biscuits are golden brown. Remove the biscuits from the oven and brush 2 tablespoons melted butter across the top of the biscuits.

Cheese Angel Biscuits

Makes 20 biscuits

1 pkg. active dry yeast
2 tbs. plus 1 tsp. granulated sugar
2 tbs. warm water
1 cup buttermilk
3 cups self rising flour
1 tsp. baking powder
3/4 tsp. baking soda
1/3 cup vegetable shortening
1 cup shredded sharp cheddar cheese

In a small bowl, add the yeast, 1 teaspoon granulated sugar and warm water. Stir until combined and let the yeast sit for 5 minutes. Add the buttermilk to the bowl and stir until combined.

In a large mixing bowl, add the self rising flour, baking powder, baking soda and 2 tablespoons granulated sugar. Stir until combined and add the vegetable shortening to the bowl. Using a pastry blender, cut the shortening into the dry ingredients until you have coarse crumbs. Add the yeast mixture and cheddar cheese to the bowl. Stir until the dough is moistened and combined.

Cover the bowl and refrigerate the dough for 30 minutes. Lightly flour your work surface. Place the dough on your surface and knead 5 times or until the dough holds together. Roll the dough to 1/2" thickness. Using a 2 1/2" biscuit cutter, cut out the biscuits. Cut the biscuits as close together as possible to get as many biscuits as you can on the first cutting. Roll the dough scraps out and cut out the remaining biscuits if needed.

Spray two baking sheets with non stick cooking spray. Place the biscuits on the baking sheets. Space the biscuits about 2" apart. Loosely cover the biscuits and let the biscuits rise in a warm place for 30 minutes.

Preheat the oven to 400°. Bake the biscuits for 10-12 minutes or until the biscuits are golden brown. Remove the biscuits from the oven and serve hot.

Sweet Potato Angel Biscuits

Unbaked biscuits can be frozen up to 1 month. Makes 7 dozen.

3 cups cooked mashed sweet potatoes, cooled
3 pkgs. active dry yeast
3/4 cup warm water
7 1/2 cups all purpose flour
1 tbs. baking powder
1 tbs. salt
1 1/2 cups granulated sugar
1 1/2 cups vegetable shortening

In a small bowl, add the yeast and warm water. Stir until combined and let the yeast sit for 5 minutes. In a large mixing bowl, add the all purpose flour, baking powder, granulated sugar and salt. Stir until combined and add the vegetable shortening to the bowl. Using a pastry blender, cut the shortening into the dry ingredients until you have coarse crumbs. Add the yeast mixture and sweet potatoes to the bowl. Stir until the dough is moistened and combined.

Cover the bowl and refrigerate the dough for 8 to 12 hours. Lightly flour your work surface. Place the dough on your surface and roll the dough to 1/2" thickness. Using a 2" biscuit cutter, cut out the biscuits. Cut the biscuits as close together as possible to get as many biscuits as you can on the first cutting. Roll the dough scraps out and cut out the remaining biscuits.

Place the biscuits on ungreased baking sheets. Space the biscuits about 2" apart. Loosely cover the biscuits with plastic wrap and let the biscuits rise in a warm place for 30 minutes. The biscuits should be doubled in size when ready.

Preheat the oven to 400°. Bake the biscuits for 10-12 minutes or until the biscuits are golden brown. Remove the biscuits from the oven and serve hot.

Freeze the unbaked biscuits up to 1 month in the freezer. Freeze the biscuits before the second rise. To cook the frozen biscuits, place the biscuits on a baking sheet. Loosely cover the biscuits with plastic wrap and let the biscuits rise in a warm place for 1 hour. The biscuits will be doubled in size when ready. Bake as directed above.

Honey Angel Biscuits

Makes 4 dozen

1 pkg. active dry yeast
2 tbs. warm water
5 cups all purpose flour
1 tbs. baking powder
1 tsp. baking soda
1 tsp. salt
1 cup vegetable shortening
1 cup buttermilk
3 tbs. honey
Honey butter, optional

In a small bowl, add the yeast and warm water. Stir until the yeast dissolves and let the yeast sit for 5 minutes. In a large mixing bowl, add the all purpose flour, baking powder, baking soda and salt. Stir until well combined and add the vegetable shortening. Using a pastry blender, cut the shortening into the dry ingredients until you have coarse crumbs. Add the yeast mixture, buttermilk and honey to the bowl. Stir only until the dough is moistened and combined.

Lightly flour your work surface. Place the dough on your surface and knead for 1 minute. The dough should be smooth and combined. Roll the dough to 1/2" thickness. Using a 2" biscuit cutter, cut out the biscuits. Cut the biscuits as close together as possible to cut as many biscuits as you can on the first cutting. Roll the dough scraps out again and cut out the remaining biscuits.

Preheat the oven to 400°. Place the biscuits on ungreased baking sheets. Space the biscuits about 2" apart. Bake for 10-12 minutes or until the biscuits are golden brown. Remove the biscuits from the oven and serve hot with honey butter. You can refrigerate the dough up to 1 week in a covered container.

Honey butter: Add 1/4 cup honey and 1/2 cup softened unsalted butter to a small bowl. Stir until well combined and serve. Store leftover butter covered in the refrigerator.

Savory Pumpkin Biscuits

Makes about 12 biscuits

2 1/3 cups all purpose flour
1 tbs. baking powder
1/4 tsp. baking soda
1/2 tsp. salt
1/8 tsp. cayenne pepper
6 tbs. cold unsalted butter
1 cup pureed cooked pumpkin
1/3 cup whole milk
2 tbs. light brown sugar
1 tbs. vegetable shortening
2 tbs. unsalted butter, melted

Preheat the oven to 425°. Grease your baking pan with the vegetable shortening. In a mixing bowl, add the all purpose flour, baking powder, baking soda, salt, cayenne pepper and brown sugar. Stir until well mixed. The brown sugar must be well combined in the dry ingredients.

Add 6 tablespoons cold butter. Using a pastry blender, cut the butter into the dry ingredients until you have coarse crumbs. Add the pumpkin and milk to the bowl. Mix only until the dough is moistened and combined.

Lightly flour your work surface. Place the dough on the work surface. Do not add additional flour unless needed to make a soft dough that holds together. Flatten the dough with your hand. Fold the dough in half and flatten the dough again. Repeat 2 more times. Do not over work the dough or the biscuits will be tough.

Pat the dough out to a 3/4" thickness. Using a 2" biscuit cutter, cut out the biscuits and place each biscuit on the baking sheet. Roll the scraps of dough again and cut out the remaining biscuits. Bake for 13-16 minutes or until the biscuits are golden brown. Remove the biscuits from the oven and brush 2 tablespoons melted butter across the top of the biscuits.

Browned Butter and Sage Biscuits

Makes about 12 biscuits

6 tbs. unsalted butter
2 tbs. fresh sage, chopped
1 tsp. fresh thyme, chopped
2 cups all purpose flour
1 tbs. baking powder
1 tbs. granulated sugar
3/4 tsp. salt
3/4 cup whole milk
2 tbs. unsalted butter, melted
1 tbs. vegetable shortening

Run about 3" cold water in your sink. It is very important to brown the butter for the biscuits but do not burn the butter. There is a fine line between browned butter and burnt butter so watch the cooking closely.

In a heavy sauce pan over medium heat, add 6 tablespoons butter. Stir constantly and let the butter melt. The butter will begin to brown on the bottom or the sides of the pan when ready. This will only take a couple of minutes so watch the butter closely. When the butter begins to brown, remove the pan from the heat and place the bottom of the pan in the cold water. Add the sage and thyme. Let the herbs steep in the butter and cool the butter to room temperature.

Preheat the oven to 425°. Grease your baking pan with the vegetable shortening. In a mixing bowl, add the all purpose flour, baking powder, granulated sugar and salt. Stir until well combined. Add the butter and herbs along with the milk to the bowl. Stir only until the dough is moistened and combined.

Lightly flour your work surface. Place the dough on the work surface. Do not add additional flour unless needed to make a soft dough that holds together. Flatten the dough with your hand. Fold the dough in half and flatten the dough again. Repeat 2 more times. Do not over work the dough or the biscuits will be tough. Pat the dough out to a 3/4" thickness. Using a 2" biscuit cutter, cut out the biscuits and place each biscuit on the baking sheet. Roll the scraps of dough again and cut out the remaining biscuits. Bake for 13-16 minutes or until the biscuits are golden brown. Remove the biscuits from the oven and brush the melted butter across the top of the biscuits.

Country Ham Sour Cream Biscuits

Makes 10 biscuits

1/3 cup unsalted butter
2 cups self rising flour
1/4 cup whole milk
1 cup sour cream
1 cup cooked country ham, ground
2 tbs. unsalted butter, melted

Preheat the oven to 425°. In a mixing bowl, add 1/3 cup butter and self rising flour. Using a pastry blender, cut the butter into the flour until you have coarse crumbs. Add the milk, sour cream and ham to the bowl. Stir until well combined and a soft dough forms.

Lightly flour your work surface. Place the dough on the work surface. With the palm of your hand, slightly flatten the dough. Fold the dough over and slightly flatten the dough again. Turn the dough about 1/4 turn and fold the dough over again. Repeat two more times. The dough should be smooth and soft.

Pat the dough to a 1/2" thickness with your hands. Using a 2 1/2" biscuit cutter, cut out the biscuits. Lightly pat out the dough scraps again to cut out all the biscuits. Place the biscuits on your baking sheet. Bake for 10-12 minutes or until the biscuits are done and lightly browned. Remove the biscuits from the oven and brush 2 tablespoons melted butter over the biscuits before serving. Serve the biscuits hot.

Country Ham & Swiss Biscuits

Makes 12 biscuits

2 cups self rising flour
1/4 cup vegetable shortening, chilled
1 cup finely chopped country ham
1 cup shredded Swiss cheese
1 cup sour cream
1/4 cup whole milk
2 tbs. unsalted butter, melted
1 tbs. vegetable shortening

Preheat the oven to 450°. Grease your baking pan with 1 tablespoon vegetable shortening. In a mixing bowl, add the self rising flour and 1/4 cup vegetable shortening. Using a pastry blender, cut the shortening into the flour until you have coarse crumbs.

Add the ham, Swiss cheese, sour cream and milk to the bowl. Mix only until the dough is moistened and combined.

Lightly flour your work surface. Place the dough on the work surface. Do not add additional flour unless needed to make a soft dough that holds together. Flatten the dough with your hand. Fold the dough in half and flatten the dough again. Repeat 2 more times. Do not over work the dough or the biscuits will be tough.

Pat the dough out to a 3/4" thickness. Using a 2" biscuit cutter, cut out the biscuits and place each biscuit on the baking sheet. Roll the scraps of dough again and cut out the remaining biscuits. Bake for 13-16 minutes or until the biscuits are golden brown. Remove the biscuits from the oven and brush the melted butter across the top of the biscuits.

Onion Cheddar Filled Cornmeal Biscuits

Makes 12 biscuits

1 1/2 cups all purpose flour
1/2 cup plain white or yellow cornmeal
1 tbs. baking powder
1/2 tsp. salt
1/3 cup cold vegetable shortening
1/2 cup sour cream
1/2 cup whole milk
4 oz. cheddar cheese block, cut into 12 cubes
2 tbs. chopped green onions
2 tbs. unsalted butter, melted
1 tbs. vegetable shortening

Preheat the oven to 450°. Grease your baking pan with 1 tablespoon vegetable shortening. In a mixing bowl, add the all purpose flour, cornmeal, baking powder, salt and green onions. Stir until well combined.

Add 1/3 cup cold vegetable shortening. Using a pastry blender, cut the shortening into the dry ingredients until you have coarse crumbs. Add the milk and sour cream to the bowl. Stir only until the dough is moistened and combined.

Lightly flour your work surface. Place the dough on the work surface. Do not add additional flour unless needed to make a soft dough that holds together. Flatten the dough with your hand. Fold the dough in half and flatten the dough again. Repeat 2 more times. Do not over work the dough or the biscuits will be tough.

Pat the dough out to a 3/4" thickness. Using a 2" biscuit cutter, cut out the biscuits and place each biscuit on the baking sheet. Roll the scraps of dough again and cut out the remaining biscuits. Stuff a cheese cube in the center of each biscuit. Bake for 13-16 minutes or until the biscuits are golden brown. Remove the biscuits from the oven and brush the melted butter across the top of the biscuits.

Ham Cheddar Biscuits

Makes 12 biscuits

2 cups all purpose flour
2 tsp. baking powder
1 tsp. baking soda
1/2 tsp. salt
1/8 tsp. dry mustard
1/8 tsp. onion powder
4 tbs. unsalted butter, chilled
1/2 cup cooked finely diced ham
1/2 cup shredded cheddar cheese
1 cup whole milk
2 tbs. unsalted butter, melted
1 tbs. vegetable shortening

Preheat the oven to 450°. Grease your baking sheet with the vegetable shortening. In a mixing bowl, add the all purpose flour, baking powder, baking soda, salt, dry mustard and onion powder. Stir until well combined.

Using a pastry blender, cut 4 tablespoons butter into the dry ingredients until you have coarse crumbs. Add the ham, cheddar cheese and milk to the bowl. Stir only until the dough is moistened and combined. You may need to add a tablespoon or two of additional milk to make a moist dough.

Lightly flour your work surface. Place the dough on the work surface. Do not add additional flour unless needed to make a soft dough that holds together. Flatten the dough with your hand. Fold the dough in half and flatten the dough again. Repeat 2 more times. Do not over work the dough or the biscuits will be tough.

Pat the dough out to a 3/4" thickness. Using a 2" biscuit cutter, cut out the biscuits and place each biscuit on the baking sheet. Roll the scraps of dough again and cut out the remaining biscuits. Bake for 13-16 minutes or until the biscuits are golden brown. Remove the biscuits from the oven and brush the melted butter across the top of the biscuits.

Honey Mustard Biscuits with Ham

Makes 12 biscuits

3 cups self rising flour
2/3 cup whole milk
1/2 cup unsalted butter, cold
1/4 cup Dijon honey mustard
1 1/2 lbs. ham slices, cooked
2 tbs. unsalted butter, melted
1 tbs. vegetable shortening

Preheat the oven to 450°. Grease your baking sheet with the vegetable shortening. In a mixing bowl, add the self rising flour and 1/2 cup butter. Using a pastry blender, cut the butter into the flour until you have coarse crumbs. Add the milk and honey mustard to the bowl. Stir until the dough is moistened and combined.

Lightly flour your work surface. Place the dough on the work surface. Do not add additional flour unless needed to make a soft dough that holds together. Flatten the dough with your hand. Fold the dough in half and flatten the dough again. Repeat 2 more times. Do not over work the dough or the biscuits will be tough.

Pat the dough out to a 3/4" thickness. Using a 2" biscuit cutter, cut out the biscuits and place each biscuit on the baking sheet. Roll the scraps of dough again and cut out the remaining biscuits. Bake for 13-16 minutes or until the biscuits are golden brown. Remove the biscuits from the oven and brush the melted butter across the top of the biscuits. Split the biscuits open and serve with ham slices for a biscuit sandwich.

Bacon Ranch Biscuits

Makes about 12-16 biscuits

3 cups all purpose flour
2 1/2 tsp. baking powder
1/2 tsp. baking soda
1 tsp. salt
2 tbs. onion powder
1/2 tsp. garlic powder
2 tbs. fresh minced chives
3/4 cup crumbled and cooked bacon
1 tbs. granulated sugar
1/2 cup unsalted butter, cold
1 egg
1 cup buttermilk
1 tbs. vegetable shortening
2 tbs. unsalted butter, melted

Preheat the oven to 425°. Grease your baking pan with vegetable shortening. In a mixing bowl, add the all purpose flour, baking powder, baking soda, salt, onion powder, garlic powder, bacon, granulated sugar and chives. Stir until well blended.

Using a pastry blender, cut 1/2 cup cold butter into the dry ingredients until you have coarse crumbs. In a separate bowl, add the egg and buttermilk. Mix until well combined and add to the dry ingredients. Mix only until the dough is moistened and combined.

Lightly flour your work surface. Place the dough on the work surface. Do not add additional flour unless needed to make a soft dough that holds together. Flatten the dough with your hand. Fold the dough in half and flatten the dough again. Repeat 2 more times. Do not over work the dough or the biscuits will be tough.

Pat the dough out to a 3/4" thickness. Using a 2" biscuit cutter, cut out the biscuits and place each biscuit on the baking sheet. Roll the scraps of dough again and cut out the remaining biscuits. Bake for 16-20 minutes or until the biscuits are golden brown. Remove the biscuits from the oven and brush the melted butter across the top of the biscuits.

Cracklin' Biscuits

Makes 12 biscuits

2 cups self rising flour
1/3 cup unsalted butter, chilled
1/2 cup cracklin's
3/4 to 1 cup whole milk
2 tbs. unsalted butter, melted
1 tbs. vegetable shortening

Preheat the oven to 425°. Grease your baking sheet with 1 tablespoon vegetable shortening. In a mixing bowl, add the self rising flour and 1/3 cup butter. Using a pastry blender, cut the butter into the flour until you have coarse crumbs. Add the cracklin's and stir until combined. Add 3/4 cup milk and stir only until the batter is moistened and combined. Add the remaining milk if needed to make a soft dough.

Lightly flour your work surface. Place the dough on the work surface. Do not add additional flour unless needed to make a soft dough that holds together. Flatten the dough with your hand. Fold the dough in half and flatten the dough again. Repeat 2 more times. Do not over work the dough or the biscuits will be tough.

Pat the dough out to a 3/4" thickness. Using a 2" biscuit cutter, cut out the biscuits and place each biscuit on the baking sheet. Roll the scraps of dough again and cut out the remaining biscuits. Bake for 13-16 minutes or until the biscuits are golden brown. Remove the biscuits from the oven and brush the melted butter across the top of the biscuits.

Sage & Cheddar Cornmeal Biscuits

Makes 12 biscuits

1 1/2 cups all purpose flour
1/2 cup self rising cornmeal
2 tsp. granulated sugar
3/4 tsp. rubbed sage
2 tsp. baking powder
1/2 tsp. salt
1/2 cup vegetable shortening, chilled
3/4 to 1 cup whole milk
1/2 cup shredded sharp cheddar cheese
2 tbs. unsalted butter, melted
1 tbs. vegetable shortening

Preheat the oven to 425°. Grease your baking sheet with 1 tablespoon vegetable shortening. In a mixing bowl, add the all purpose flour, cornmeal, granulated sugar, sage, baking powder and salt. Stir until well blended.

Add the vegetable shortening to the dry ingredients. Using a pastry blender, cut the vegetable shortening into the dry ingredients. Add 3/4 cup milk and the cheddar cheese to the bowl. Stir only until the dough is moistened and combined. Add the remaining milk if needed to make a soft dough.

Lightly flour your work surface. Place the dough on the work surface. Do not add additional flour unless needed to make a soft dough that holds together. Flatten the dough with your hand. Fold the dough in half and flatten the dough again. Repeat 2 more times. Do not over work the dough or the biscuits will be tough.

Pat the dough out to a 3/4" thickness. Using a 2" biscuit cutter, cut out the biscuits and place each biscuit on the baking sheet. Roll the scraps of dough again and cut out the remaining biscuits. Bake for 13-16 minutes or until the biscuits are golden brown. Remove the biscuits from the oven and brush the melted butter across the top of the biscuits.

Caramelized Onion & Bacon Biscuits

Makes 12 biscuits

10 tbs. cold unsalted butter
2 onions, chopped
2 1/2 cups all purpose flour
1 tbs. baking powder
1/2 tsp. salt
3/4 cup whole milk
1/2 cup cooked and crumbled bacon

Preheat the oven to 400°. In a skillet over medium heat, add 3 tablespoons butter and the onions. Stir constantly and cook the onions about 5-6 minutes or until they are brown and tender. Remove the pan from the heat and set aside while you prepare the dough. If the onions are browning too fast, turn the heat down to low.

In a mixing bowl, add the all purpose flour, baking powder and salt. Add 5 tablespoons cold butter to the dry ingredients. Using a pastry blender, cut the butter into the dry ingredients. The dough should resemble coarse crumbs.

Add the cooked onion along with any butter left in the sauce pan to the bowl. Add the milk and bacon to the dough. Mix only until the dough is moistened and combined. You will have a soft dough that is sticky but not gooey.

Lightly flour your work surface. Place the dough on your surface. Fold the dough in half and then in half again, rotating the dough slightly each time you fold. Repeat this process three or four times to form layers. Pat the dough out to 1/2" thickness. Using a 2" biscuit cutter, cut the biscuits from the dough. Roll the dough scraps and cut out the remaining biscuits.

Grease a baking sheet with 1 tablespoon butter. Place the biscuits on the greased baking pan. Bake for 12-15 minutes or until the biscuits are done and golden brown. Remove the biscuits from the oven. Melt 1 tablespoon butter in the microwave. Brush the melted butter over the top of the biscuits.

Bacon and Chive Biscuits

Makes 12-15 biscuits

3 cups all purpose flour
1/2 cup shredded sharp cheddar cheese
4 1/2 tsp. baking powder
1/2 tsp. salt
1 tbs. granulated sugar
7 tbs. unsalted butter
3 tbs. fresh snipped chives
6 slices slab bacon, cooked and finely chopped
1 1/4 cups whole milk
1 tbs. bacon drippings, melted

Preheat the oven to 425°. Grease a baking pan with 1 tablespoon butter. In a mixing bowl, add the all purpose flour, cheddar cheese, baking powder, salt, granulated sugar and 6 tablespoons butter. Using a pastry blender, cut the butter in the dry ingredients until you have coarse crumbs. Add the chives, bacon crumbles, milk and the melted bacon drippings to the bowl. Stir until well combined and the dough is moistened.

Lightly flour your work surface. Place the dough on the work surface. Fold the dough in half and then in half again, rotating the dough slightly each time you fold. Repeat this process three or four times to form layers. Pat the dough out to 1/2" thickness. Using a 2 1/2" biscuit cutter, cut the biscuits from the dough. Roll the dough scraps and cut out the remaining biscuits.

Place the biscuits on the prepared pan and bake for 12-15 minutes or until golden brown. Remove the biscuits from the oven and serve hot.

Sour Cream Chive Biscuits

Makes 12 biscuits

2 cups all purpose flour
1 tbs. baking powder
1/2 tsp. salt
1/4 tsp. baking soda
1/3 cup vegetable shortening
3/4 cup sour cream
1/4 cup whole milk
1/4 cup fresh chopped chives

Preheat the oven to 400°. In a mixing bowl, add the all purpose flour, baking powder, baking soda and salt. Stir until well combined. Add the shortening to the bowl. Using a pastry blender, cut the shortening into the dry ingredients until you have coarse crumbs.

Add the sour cream, milk and chives to the bowl. Mix only until combined and a dough forms. Lightly flour your work surface. Place the dough on the floured work surface. Pat the dough out to 1/2" thickness. Fold the dough in half and then in half again, rotating the dough slightly each time you fold. Repeat this process three or four times to form layers.

Pat the dough to 3/4" thickness. Using a 2" biscuit cutter, cut out the biscuits and place them on an ungreased baking sheet. Roll the dough scraps and cut out the remaining biscuits. Bake for 12-15 minutes or until the biscuits are done and golden brown. Remove the biscuits from the oven and serve hot.

Green Onion & Pepper Biscuits

These biscuits will not rise high like regular biscuits. They will rise but do not expect mile high biscuits. They are so good with a slice of fried ham. Makes about 12-15 biscuits.

2 1/2 cups all purpose flour
1 tsp. baking powder
1 1/2 tsp. salt
1 tsp. black pepper
1 tsp. cayenne pepper
1/4 tsp. baking soda
1/2 cup unsalted butter, chilled
1 1/4 cups sliced green onions
2 eggs, beaten
2/3 cup sour cream
1 tbs. melted unsalted butter

Preheat the oven to 400°. Grease a baking pan with 1 tablespoon melted butter. In a mixing bowl, add the all purpose flour, baking powder, salt, black pepper, cayenne pepper, baking soda and 1/2 cup butter. Using your fingers, work the butter into the dry ingredients until you have coarse crumbs. Add the green onions, eggs and sour cream to the bowl. Mix only until combined and a soft dough forms.

Lightly flour your work surface. Place the dough on the floured work surface. Fold the dough in half and then in half again, rotating the dough slightly each time you fold. Repeat this process three or four times to form layers.

Pat the dough to about 1/2" thickness. Using a 2" biscuit cutter, cut out the biscuits and place them on the prepared pan. Roll the dough scraps and cut out the remaining biscuits. Bake for 15-20 minutes or until the biscuits are done and golden brown. Remove the biscuits from the oven and serve hot.

Spicy Pepper Jack Biscuits

Makes 12 - 14 biscuits

2 1/4 cups all purpose flour
4 tsp. baking powder
1/2 tsp. salt
1/4 tsp. baking soda
1 tbs. granulated sugar
1 tsp. cayenne pepper
1 cup shredded Pepper Jack cheese
7 tbs. unsalted butter
3/4 to 1 cup whole milk
3 tbs. unsalted butter, melted

Preheat the oven to 425°. Spread 1 tablespoon melted butter on a baking pan. In a mixing bowl, add the all purpose flour, baking powder, salt, baking soda, granulated sugar, cayenne pepper and 7 tablespoons butter. Using a pastry blender, cut the butter into the dry ingredients until you have coarse crumbs.

Add the Pepper Jack cheese and 3/4 cup milk to the bowl. Stir until the dough is moistened, combined and forms into a ball. Add the remaining 1/4 cup milk, in tablespoon increments, if need to form a soft dough.

Lightly flour your work surface. Place the dough on the work surface. Fold the dough in half and then in half again, rotating the dough slightly each time you fold. Repeat this process three or four times to form layers. Pat the dough out to 1/2" thickness. Using a 2" biscuit cutter, cut out the biscuits. Place the biscuits on the prepared pan. Roll the dough scraps and cut out the remaining biscuits. Bake for 12-15 minutes or until the biscuits are done and golden brown.

Brush the biscuits with 2 tablespoons melted butter when they are fresh out of the oven.

Chive Whole Wheat Drop Biscuits

Makes 12 biscuits

1 1/4 cups whole wheat flour
3/4 cup all purpose flour
3 tbs. toasted wheat germ
1 tbs. baking powder
1 tbs. chopped fresh chives
2 tsp. granulated sugar
3 tbs. unsalted butter
1 cup whole milk
1/4 cup shredded American cheese

Preheat the oven to 450°. Spray a baking sheet with non stick cooking spray. In a mixing bowl, add the whole wheat flour, all purpose flour, 2 tablespoons wheat germ, baking powder, chives and granulated sugar. Stir until well combined. Add the butter to the dry ingredients. Using a pastry blender, cut the butter into the dry ingredients until you have coarse crumbs. Add the milk and American cheese to the bowl. Stir only until the dough is moistened and combined.

Drop the dough by teaspoonfuls onto the baking sheets. Space the biscuits about 1" apart on the baking sheet. Sprinkle the remaining 1 tablespoon wheat germ over the biscuits. Bake for 12 minutes or until the biscuits are golden brown. A toothpick inserted in the biscuits will come out clean when ready. Remove the biscuits from the oven and serve.

Parmesan Pepper Biscuit Sticks

Makes 2 dozen

2 cups all purpose flour
1 tbs. baking powder
1/2 tsp. baking soda
1 tsp. black pepper
2/3 cup grated Parmesan cheese
3 tbs. unsalted butter, chilled
1 cup whole milk
2 tbs. unsalted butter, melted

Preheat the oven to 450°. In a mixing bowl, add the all purpose flour, baking powder, baking soda, black pepper and Parmesan cheese. Stir until well combined and add 3 tablespoons butter to the bowl. Using a pastry blender, cut the butter into the dry ingredients until you have coarse crumbs. Add the milk and stir only until a soft dough forms and the dough leaves the sides of the bowl.

Lightly flour your work surface. Place the dough on your surface and knead 5 times. Roll the dough into a 12" x 9" rectangle. Spray your baking sheets with non stick cooking spray. Cut the dough into 3" x 1 1/2" rectangles. Cut each rectangle in half. Place the biscuits on the baking sheets.

Brush 2 tablespoons melted butter over the biscuits. Bake for 10 minutes or until the biscuits are lightly browned. Remove the biscuits from the oven and serve.

Southern Homemade Biscuits

Makes about 10-12 biscuits

1/2 cup cold unsalted butter
3 tsp. baking powder
1/2 tsp. salt
2 cups all purpose flour
1 tsp. granulated sugar
3/4 – 1 cup whole milk
2 tbs. melted unsalted butter
1 tbs. vegetable shortening

Preheat the oven to 450°. The oven should heat at least 10 minutes before placing the biscuits in the oven. Lightly grease your baking pan with the vegetable shortening. The closer biscuits are together in a pan, the better they will rise. Try not to use a larger than necessary pan.

In a mixing bowl, add the all purpose flour, baking powder, salt and the granulated sugar. Stir until well combined. Cut 1/2 cup cold butter into small squares. With a pastry blender, cut the butter into the dry ingredients until the butter is no larger than small peas. You should be able to see the butter in the dough after you have finished cutting in the butter.

Add 3/4 cup milk and stir until the dough leaves the sides of the bowl and begins to hold together. You may need to add the additional 1/4 cup milk to make a soft dough. The dough will be soft and slightly sticky.

Turn the dough onto a floured surface. I do not use a rolling pin. Pat the dough into a circle with your hands about 1/2" thick. Add just enough flour to keep the dough from sticking to your hands. Fold the dough in half and then in half again, rotating the dough slightly each time you fold. Repeat this process four times to form layers. Pat the dough to 1/2" thickness.

Using a sharp 2 1/2" biscuit cutter, cut out the biscuits. Do not twist the biscuit cutter when cutting out the dough. Press straight down on the biscuit cutter. Cut the biscuits close together so you can cut out as many as possible on the first rolling. Place the cut biscuits on your baking sheet with the sides of each biscuit touching. Pat out the dough scraps and cut out the remaining biscuits.

Brush the biscuits with 1 tablespoon melted butter and place them in the freezer for 5 minutes. Remove the biscuits from the freezer and bake for 12-15 minutes or until the biscuits are golden brown and fluffy. Depending upon your oven, it may take an additional few minutes to bake the biscuits. I know it is tempting to open the oven door to see the biscuits rise, but do not open the oven before 10 minutes.

When the biscuits are done, remove them from the oven and brush the top and sides with 1 tablespoon melted butter.

Old Fashioned Buttermilk Biscuits

Makes 15 biscuits

4 cups all purpose flour
2 tbs. baking powder
1 tsp. baking soda
3/4 tsp. salt
1 tbs. granulated sugar
1 1/2 cups buttermilk
2/3 cup unsalted butter
1/4 cup unsalted butter, melted
1 tbs. lard or vegetable shortening

Preheat the oven to 450°. Grease your iron skillet or baking pan with the lard or vegetable shortening. In a mixing bowl, add the all purpose flour, baking powder, baking soda, salt and granulated sugar. Stir until well combined and add 2/3 cup butter to the dry ingredients. Using a pastry blender, cut the butter into the dry ingredients until you have coarse crumbs. Add the buttermilk and stir only until the dough is moistened and combined. You should have a soft dough at this point.

Lightly flour your work surface. Place the dough on your surface. Knead the dough four or five times by folding and flattening the dough with your hands each time. Be gentle with the dough and do not over knead or the biscuits will be tough. Pat the dough out to about 3/4" thick. Using a 2 1/2" biscuit cutter, cut out the biscuits and on place them on the prepared pan. Cut the biscuits as close together as possible to get as many as you can on the first rolling. Flatten the remaining dough to 3/4" thickness again and cut out the remaining biscuits.

Brush the top of the biscuits with melted butter. Bake for 12-15 minutes or until golden brown. Serve hot.

Cloud Biscuits

Makes 12 biscuits

2 1/4 cups self rising flour
1 tbs. granulated sugar
1/2 cup butter flavored shortening
1 egg, beaten
2/3 cup whole milk
1 tbs. unsalted butter, melted

In a mixing bowl, add the self rising flour and granulated sugar. Stir until combined and add the shortening. Using a pastry blender, cut the shortening into the flour mixture until you have coarse crumbs.

In a small bowl, add the egg and milk. Whisk until combined and add to the dry ingredients. Stir only until a soft dough forms and the dough leaves the sides of the bowl.

Lightly flour your work surface. Place the dough on your work surface and knead the dough 4 times. Roll the dough to 1/2" thickness. Using a 2 1/2" biscuit cutter, cut out the biscuits. Cut the biscuits as close together as possible on the first cutting. Roll the dough scraps out again and cut out the remaining biscuits.

Place the biscuits on an ungreased baking sheet. Bake for 12 minutes or until the biscuits are golden brown. Remove the biscuits from the oven and brush the melted butter over the biscuits. Serve the biscuits hot.

Refrigerator Cream Cheese Biscuits

Makes 2 dozen mini muffin biscuits. You can store the dough up to 3 days covered in the refrigerator. Add 1 to 1 1/2 tablespoons of your favorite dried herb to the batter for savory biscuits.

8 oz. cream cheese, softened
1/2 cup unsalted butter, softened
1 cup self rising flour

Add the cream cheese and butter to a mixing bowl. Using a mixer on medium speed, beat for 2 minutes. The mixture should be creamy and combined. Turn the mixer to low and add the self rising flour. Mix only until blended.

Spray a miniature muffin tin with non stick cooking spray. Spray the muffin tin well or the biscuits will stick to the pan. Spoon the batter into the muffin tins filling them about 2/3 full. Preheat the oven to 400°. Bake for 15 minutes or until the biscuits are golden brown. Immediately remove the biscuits from the muffin tins and serve.

Rosemary Cream Cheese Biscuits

Makes 2 dozen biscuits

3 oz. pkg. cream cheese, softened
1 3/4 cups Bisquick
1/2 cup whole milk
2 tbs. chopped fresh rosemary

Add the cream cheese and Bisquick to a mixing bowl. Using a fork, cut the cream cheese into the Bisquick until you have coarse crumbs. Add the milk and rosemary to the bowl. Stir only until the dough is moistened and combined.

Lightly flour your work surface. Place the dough on your surface and knead the dough 4 times. The dough should be smooth. Pat the dough to 3/4" thickness. Using a 1" biscuit cutter, cut out the biscuits. Cut the biscuits as close together as possible on the first cutting. Roll the dough scraps again and cut out the remaining biscuits.

Preheat the oven to 400°. Place the biscuits on a baking sheet. Bake for 10 minutes or until the biscuits are golden brown. Remove the biscuits from the oven and serve hot.

Cream Cheese and Olive Biscuits

Makes 25 appetizer servings

2 1/4 cups Bisquick
3 oz. pkg. cream cheese, softened
1/2 cup green olives, chopped
1/3 cup whole milk

In a mixing bowl, add all the ingredients to a food processor. Process until combined and a dough forms. Lightly flour your work surface. Place the dough on your surface and pat the dough out to 1/2" thickness. Using a 2" biscuit cutter, cut out the biscuits. Cut the biscuits as close as possible to cut out as many biscuits as possible on the first cutting. Pat the dough out again and cut out the remaining biscuits.

Preheat the oven to 425°. Place the biscuits on an ungreased baking sheet. Bake for 10-12 minutes or until the biscuits are golden brown. Remove the biscuits from the oven and serve hot.

These are great with ham, bacon or most any savory spread.

Velvet Cream Biscuits

Makes about 28 biscuits

4 cups all purpose flour
2 tbs. baking powder
1 tsp. salt
2 tbs. granulated sugar
2 1/2 cups heavy whipping cream
1/4 cup plus 2 tbs. unsalted butter, melted

Preheat the oven to 425°. In a mixing bowl, add the all purpose flour, baking powder, salt and granulated sugar. Stir until combined. Add the heavy cream to the bowl. Mix until the dough is moistened and combined. You should have a soft and sticky dough.

Heavily flour your work surface. Place the dough on your surface. Knead the dough 12 times. Roll the dough to 1/2" thickness. Using a 2" biscuit cutter, cut the biscuits from the dough. Cut the biscuits as close together as possible to cut out as many as you can on the first rolling. Roll the dough scraps again and cut out the remaining biscuits.

Grease your baking sheets with 2 tablespoons melted butter. Place the biscuits on the baking sheet with the sides lightly touching each other. Brush 1/4 cup melted butter over the biscuits. Bake for 14 minutes or until the biscuits are golden brown. Remove the biscuits from the oven and serve hot.

Oatmeal Biscuits

Makes 12 biscuits

1 2/3 cups quick oats
1 1/2 cups all purpose flour
1/4 cup light brown sugar
1 tbs. plus 1 tsp. baking powder
1/2 tsp. baking soda
1/8 tsp. salt
1/4 cup vegetable shortening, chilled
1 cup buttermilk or whole milk

Preheat the oven to 450°. In a mixing bowl, add 1 1/3 cups oats, all purpose flour, brown sugar, baking powder, baking soda and salt. Stir until well combined. Add the vegetable shortening to the dry ingredients. Using a pastry blender, cut the shortening into the dry ingredients until you have coarse crumbs.

Add the buttermilk to the dry ingredients. Stir only until the dough is moistened and combined. The dough will begin to leave the sides of the bowl when ready. Shape the dough into a ball.

Lightly flour your work surface. You should have 1/3 cup oats left. Sprinkle half of the 1/3 cup oats over the dough. Pat the dough to 1/2" thickness. Sprinkle the remaining oats over the dough. Using a 2 1/2" biscuit cutter, cut out the biscuits. Cut the biscuits as close together as possible to cut out as many biscuits as possible on the first cutting. It is very important when you cut out biscuits, that you do not twist the biscuit cutter. Push straight down and do not twist the cutter. Pat the leftover dough out again and cut out the remaining biscuits.

Place the biscuits, with the sides lightly touching, on an ungreased baking sheet. Bake for 14 minutes or until the biscuits are done and golden brown. Remove the biscuits from the oven and serve hot with your favorite butter.

Sweet Potato Biscuits

Makes 8-10 biscuits

1 1/4 cups all purpose flour
2 tsp. baking powder
1 tbs. granulated sugar
1/2 tsp. salt
1/4 cup plus 1 tbs. vegetable shortening
1 cup cold cooked sweet potatoes
2-4 tbs. whole milk

Preheat the oven to 400°. Lightly grease a baking sheet with 1 tablespoon shortening. In a mixing bowl, sift together the all purpose flour, baking powder, granulated sugar and salt. Add 1/4 cup vegetable shortening to the dry ingredients. Using a pastry blender, cut the shortening into the dry ingredients until you have coarse crumbs. Add the sweet potatoes and milk to the bowl. You only want to add enough milk to make a dough that holds together. Start with 2 tablespoons milk and then add the remaining milk as needed.

Lightly flour your work surface. Place the dough on the surface and roll the dough to 1/2" thickness. Cut the biscuits out with a 2" biscuit cutter and place on the baking sheet. Cut the biscuits as close together as possible to get as many biscuits as you can on the first cutting. Roll the dough scraps together and cut out the remaining biscuits. Place the biscuits on your baking sheet. Bake for 12-15 minutes or until the biscuits are done and begin to brown. Brush the biscuits with butter if desired.

Raised Biscuits

Makes 1 dozen biscuits

1 pkg. active dry yeast
1 tbs. granulated sugar
2 tbs. warm water
2 cups self rising flour
3 tbs. lard or vegetable shortening
2/3 cup whole milk

In a small bowl, add the yeast, granulated sugar and warm water. Stir until combined and let the yeast sit for 5 minutes. In a large mixing bowl, add the self rising flour and 2 tablespoons lard. Using a pastry blender, cut the lard into the dry ingredients until you have coarse crumbs. Add the milk and yeast mixture to the bowl. Stir until the dough is moistened and combined. The dough should begin to form a ball and pulls away from the side of the bowl.

Grease your baking sheet with the remaining tablespoon of lard or vegetable shortening. Lightly flour your hands and gather about a tablespoon of the dough in your hands. Roll the dough into 1 1/2" balls. Place the balls on your prepared baking sheet. Place the dough about 2" apart on the baking sheet. Let the dough rise in a warm place about an hour or until doubled in size.

Preheat the oven to 425°. The oven needs to preheat at least 10 minutes. Place the biscuits in the oven and bake for 12-15 minutes or until they are light brown. Brush with additional melted butter if desired.

Wild Rice Cheese Biscuits

Makes 10 biscuits

2 1/4 cups Bisquick
3/4 cup whole milk
1 cup shredded cheddar cheese
2/3 cup cooked wild rice, chopped
1 tbs. unsalted butter

Preheat the oven to 425°. Grease your baking sheet with butter. In a mixing bowl, add the Bisquick, milk and cheddar cheese. Stir until the dough is moistened. Add the wild rice and stir until the dough is well combined

Drop the dough by tablespoonfuls onto the baking sheet. Space the biscuits about 2" apart on the baking sheet. Bake for 10 minutes or until a toothpick inserted in the center of the biscuits comes out clean. Remove the biscuits from the oven and serve hot.

Skillet Biscuit Bread

This is a simple and old recipe. It is a quick way to make a biscuit type bread. Cook in an iron skillet for best results. You can add 1/2 cup of your favorite cheese and dried herbs to the batter for numerous flavor combinations. Makes a 9" skillet.

2 cups self rising flour
1 cup whole milk
1/2 cup vegetable oil
2 tbs. vegetable shortening

Preheat the oven to 400°. Add the vegetable shortening to a 9" cast iron skillet. Place the skillet in the oven until the shortening melts and the skillet is hot. In a mixing bowl, add the self rising flour, milk and vegetable oil. Whisk only until the batter is smooth and combined. If you added cheese or herbs to the batter, you may need to add a tablespoon or two additional milk to make a thick batter. Pour the batter into the skillet.

Bake for 18 minutes or until the bread is done and golden brown. Remove the bread from the oven and cut into wedges. Serve the bread hot with butter or use the bread to serve with hearty soups.

Beer Biscuits

The men in the family love to make these biscuits into mile high breakfast sandwiches. They add bacon, sausage, ham, a fried egg and a slice of American cheese. They are also very good with soups, chili or stews. Makes 12 biscuits.

2 1/4 cups all purpose flour
2 1/2 teaspoons baking powder
1/4 tsp. baking soda
1/2 tsp. salt
2 tbs. granulated sugar
3/4 cup beer
1 tbs. melted unsalted butter
6 tbs. cold unsalted butter
2 tbs. whole milk

Preheat the oven to 375°. Spread 1 tablespoon melted butter on a baking pan. In a mixing bowl, add the all purpose flour, baking powder, baking soda, salt, granulated sugar and 6 tablespoons butter. Using a pastry blender, cut the butter into the dry ingredients until you have coarse crumbs.

Add the beer and mix only until a dough forms or about 1 minute. Sprinkle your work surface lightly with flour. Place the dough on the surface. Fold the dough in half and then in half again, rotating the dough slightly each time you fold. Repeat this process three or four times to form layers. Pat the dough to about 1/2" thickness. Cut the biscuits out with a 2" biscuit cutter and place on the greased pan. Roll the dough scraps and cut out the remaining biscuits.

Brush the tops and sides of the biscuits with the whole milk. Bake for 12-14 minutes or until the biscuits are done and golden brown. Remove the biscuits from the oven and serve hot.

Parmesan Pillows

Makes about 24 pieces

2 cups Bisquick
1/2 - 3/4 cup whole milk
1/2 cup unsalted butter, melted
1 cup grated Parmesan cheese
2 tbs. unsalted butter, softened

Preheat the oven to 450°. Grease your baking sheets with 2 tablespoons softened butter. In a mixing bowl, add the Bisquick and 1/2 cup milk. Stir until well combined. You need a moist but firm biscuit dough. Add the remaining milk if needed to make a firm dough.

Lightly flour your work surface. Place the dough on the work surface. Knead the dough 10 times. Only add in additional flour if needed to make a firm but soft dough. Roll the dough out to a 10 x 6 rectangle. Cut the rectangle into 2" squares. Cut each square in half. Add the melted butter to a small bowl and dip each piece in the melted butter.

Place the Parmesan cheese in a small bowl. Roll each piece in the Parmesan cheese. Place the pieces on your baking sheets. Bake for 6-10 minutes or until the biscuits are done and golden brown.

Note: You can use your favorite biscuit dough if desired instead of the Bisquick. Roll the dough out to about a 1/2" thickness if using homemade biscuit dough.

Whole Wheat Biscuits

Makes 1 dozen biscuits

1 pkg. dry yeast
2 tsp. warm water
2 1/2 cups whole wheat flour
1/2 cup all purpose flour
2 tsp. baking powder
1/2 tsp. salt
1/2 tsp. baking soda
1/4 cup unsalted butter, melted
1 tbs. honey
1 cup whole milk
2 tbs. melted butter
1 tbs. lard or vegetable shortening

Preheat the oven to 400°. Grease your baking pan with the lard or vegetable shortening. In a small bowl, add the yeast and the warm water. Stir until combined and let the yeast sit for 5 minutes.

In a large mixing bowl, add the whole wheat flour, all purpose flour, baking powder, salt and baking soda. Add 1/4 cup butter, yeast mixture, honey and milk to the bowl. Stir until all the ingredients are combined. The dough will begin to pull away from the sides of the bowl when ready.

Turn the dough out onto a lightly floured surface. Pat the dough with your hands to 1/2" thickness. With a 2" biscuit cutter, cut out the biscuits and place them on the prepared pan. Try to cut the biscuits as close together as possible to get as many as you can on the first rolling. Pat out the remaining dough and cut out the remaining biscuits.

Place the biscuits on the baking pan. Brush the biscuits with 2 tablespoons melted butter. Bake for 12-15 minutes or until golden brown. Remove the biscuits from the oven and serve hot.

Quick Cheese Biscuits

Makes 8 biscuits

2 cups Bisquick
2/3 cup whole milk
1/2 cup shredded cheddar cheese
1/4 cup unsalted butter, melted

Preheat the oven to 450°. In a mixing bowl, add the Bisquick, cheddar cheese and milk. Stir with a spoon until a dough ball forms. Sprinkle your work surface with additional Bisquick. Turn the dough onto the work surface. Knead the dough to work in additional Bisquick if the dough is too sticky. The dough needs to be moist but not gooey.

Pat the dough into a circle and flatten to about 1/2" thickness. Using a 2" biscuit cutter, cut out the biscuits. Cut the biscuits as close together as possible on the first cutting. Roll the dough scraps and cut out the remaining biscuits.

Place the biscuits on a baking sheet. Brush each biscuit with melted butter. Bake for 10-12 minutes or until the biscuits are golden brown and fluffy. Brush any remaining butter over the top of the biscuits before serving.

Note: My family loves biscuit sandwiches from these biscuits.

2 SAVORY SCONES

Scones are similar to biscuits and when properly made, are tender and fluffy. Use the recipes as a guide to creating your own savory scone recipes. Try different seasonings and finely chopped meats and cheeses to add to your scones.

Cheddar Cheese Scones

Makes 10 scones

1 1/2 cups all purpose flour
1 1/2 cups quick oats
1/4 cup light brown sugar
1 tbs. baking powder
1 tsp. cream of tartar
1/2 tsp. salt
3/4 cup sharp cheddar cheese, shredded
2/3 cup unsalted butter, melted
1/3 cup whole milk
1 egg

Preheat the oven to 425°. Spray a baking sheet with non stick cooking spray. In a mixing bowl, add the all purpose flour, oats, brown sugar, baking powder, cream of tartar, salt and cheddar cheese. Stir until well combined.

In a separate bowl, add the melted butter, milk and egg. Whisk until well combined. Pour the wet ingredients into the dry ingredients. Stir until well combined.

Lightly flour your work surface. Place the dough on the work surface and shape the dough into a ball. Do not knead or over work the dough.

Place the dough on your baking sheet. Pat the dough down to about a 1/2" thickness. You can pat the dough into a circle or a square. With a sharp knife, cut the dough into 10 pieces. Do not separate the pieces. Bake for 12-15 minutes or until the scones are done and golden brown. Remove the scones from the oven and serve hot.

Basil Parmesan Scones

Makes 8 scones

1 1/2 cups all purpose flour
1 tbs. baking powder
1/2 tsp. salt
1/4 cup chopped pine nuts
1/4 cup freshly grated Parmesan cheese
1 tsp. dried basil
1 cup heavy whipping cream

Preheat the oven to 425°. Spray your baking sheet with non stick cooking spray. Reserve 2 tablespoons of the heavy whipping cream and set aside.

In a mixing bowl, add the all purpose flour, baking powder, salt, pine nuts, Parmesan cheese and basil. Stir until well combined. Add the remaining heavy cream to the bowl. Stir only until the dough comes together and begins to form a ball. Depending upon the type of Parmesan cheese used, you may need to add a teaspoon or two of additional flour or milk to make a soft dough.

Lightly flour your work surface. Place the dough on the work surface. Softly knead the dough 3 or 4 times until it forms a soft but moist dough. Do not over knead the dough or the scones will be tough. Place the dough on your baking sheet. Pat the dough into an 8" circle. Cut the dough into 8 wedges but do no separate the scones. Brush the reserved 2 tablespoons heavy cream over the scones. Bake for 15-18 minutes or until the scones are done and lightly browned. Remove the pan from the oven and cut the scones again if needed. Serve hot.

Onion Scones

Makes 8 scones

1 onion, chopped
2 garlic cloves, minced
1/3 cup unsalted butter
2 cups all purpose flour
2 tbs. granulated sugar
1 tbs. baking powder
1/4 tsp. black pepper
1/2 tsp. salt
1/3 cup light cream
1 egg, beaten

Preheat the oven to 400°. In a skillet over medium low heat, add the onion, garlic and butter. Saute the onion and garlic for 5 minutes. Stir constantly while cooking the onion and garlic. Remove the skillet from the heat and cool for 10 minutes.

Spray your baking pan with non stick cooking spray. In a mixing bowl, add the all purpose flour, granulated sugar, baking powder, black pepper and salt. Stir until well combined. In a separate bowl, add the egg and light cream. Whisk until well combined and add the onion, garlic and butter from the skillet. Stir until well combined and add to the dry ingredients.

Stir only until the batter is combined. Lightly flour your work surface. Place the dough on the work surface and form the dough into an 8" circle. Place the dough on the baking sheet. Cut the circle into 8 wedges but do not separate the wedges. Bake for 12-15 minutes or until the scones are done and lightly browned. Remove the scones from the oven and serve hot.

Pear Asiago Scones

Makes 8 scones

2 cups all purpose flour
1 tbs. baking powder
1/2 cup cold unsalted butter, cut into small pieces
3/4 cup finely chopped fresh pear
1/2 cup grated Asiago cheese
1 tsp. chopped fresh rosemary
1 cup whipping cream

Preheat the oven to 450°. Spray a baking sheet with non stick cooking spray. In a mixing bowl, add the all purpose flour and baking powder. Stir until well combined and add the butter to the dry ingredients. Using a pastry blender, cut the butter into the dry ingredients until you have coarse crumbs. Freeze the dough for 5 minutes.

Add the pear, Asiago cheese, rosemary and 3/4 cup plus 2 tablespoons whipping cream to the dry ingredients. Stir only until the dough is moistened and combined. Lightly flour your work surface. Pat the dough into a 7" round. The dough will be crumbly. Cut the round into 8 wedges.

Place the scones on the baking sheet. Brush the remaining 2 tablespoons whipping cream over the scones. Bake for 12-15 minutes or until the scones are golden brown. Remove the scones from the oven and serve hot or at room temperature.

Blue Cheese Nut Scones

Makes about 20 scones

2 cups all purpose flour
1 tbs. baking powder
2 tsp. granulated sugar
1/2 tsp. salt
1/4 cup butter flavored vegetable shortening
2 eggs, at room temperature
1/2 cup heavy cream
1/2 cup crumbled blue cheese
1/2 cup chopped pecans

Preheat the oven to 400°. In a mixing bowl, add the all purpose flour, baking powder, granulated sugar and salt. Stir until well combined. Add the vegetable shortening to the dry ingredients. Using a pastry blender, cut the shortening into the dry ingredients until you have coarse crumbs. Add the blue cheese and pecans to the dry ingredients. Stir only until combined.

In a mixing bowl, add 1 egg, 1 egg yolk and heavy cream. Whisk until well combined and add to the dry ingredients. Mix only until the dough is moistened and combined. Depending upon the brand of flour and blue cheese used, you may need to use an additional tablespoon or two heavy cream. Gently shape the dough into a ball.

Lightly flour your work surface. Place the dough on your surface and pat the dough to a 1/2" thickness. Using a 2" round biscuit cutter, cut out the scones. Cut the scones as close together as possible to cut out as many scones as possible on the first cutting. It is very important when you cut out the scones, that you do not twist the biscuit cutter. Push straight down and do not twist the cutter. Pat the leftover dough out again and cut out the remaining scones. Place the scones on an ungreased baking sheet.

In a small bowl, whisk together the remaining egg white. Brush the egg white over the scones. Bake for 10 minutes or until the scones are done and golden brown. Remove the scones from the oven and serve hot.

Cheddar Herb Scones

Makes about 18 scones

2 cups all purpose flour
1 tbs. baking powder
2 tsp. granulated sugar
1/2 tsp. salt
1/4 cup vegetable shortening
2 eggs, at room temperature
1/2 cup heavy cream
3/4 cup shredded cheddar cheese
1 tsp. dried herbs

Use your favorite dried herbs in this recipe. I like dried Italian seasoning and dried minced garlic in this recipe. Preheat the oven to 400°. In a mixing bowl, add the all purpose flour, baking powder, granulated sugar and salt. Stir until well combined and add the vegetable shortening to the dry ingredients. Using a pastry blender, cut the shortening into the dry ingredients until you have coarse crumbs. Add the cheddar cheese and herbs to the dry ingredients. Stir only until combined.

In a mixing bowl, add 1 egg, 1 egg yolk and heavy cream. Whisk until well combined and add to the dry ingredients. Mix only until the dough is moistened and combined. Depending upon the brand of flour and cheddar cheese used, you may need to use an additional tablespoon or two heavy cream. Gently shape the dough into a ball.

Lightly flour your work surface. Place the dough on your surface and pat the dough to a 1/2" thickness. Using a 2" round biscuit cutter, cut out the scones. Cut the scones as close together as possible to cut out as many scones as possible on the first cutting. It is very important when you cut out the scones, that you do not twist the biscuit cutter. Push straight down and do not twist the cutter. Pat the leftover dough out again and cut out the remaining scones. Place the scones on an ungreased baking sheet.

In a small bowl, whisk together the remaining egg white. Brush the egg white over the scones. Bake for 10 minutes or until the scones are done and golden brown. Remove the scones from the oven and serve hot.

Tabasco Parmesan Scones

Makes 8 scones

2 cups all purpose flour
3/4 cup grated Parmesan cheese
2 tsp. baking powder
1 tsp. dried oregano
1/4 tsp. salt
4 tbs. cold butter, cut into pieces
1/2 cup whole milk
2 eggs, beaten
1 tsp. Tabasco sauce
3/4 cup chopped onion

Preheat the oven to 400°. Spray a baking sheet with non stick cooking spray. In a food processor, add the all purpose flour, Parmesan cheese, baking powder, oregano, salt and butter. Process until the mixture resembles coarse crumbs. Spoon the dry ingredients into a mixing bowl.

In a separate mixing bowl, add the milk, eggs, Tabasco and onion. Whisk until well combined and add to the dry ingredients. Mix only until the dough is combined and moistened. You will have a soft but sticky dough. Place the dough in the middle of the baking sheet. With floured hands, pat the dough into a 9" circle. Cut the circle into 8 wedges with a sharp knife. Do not separate the wedges.

Bake for 20 minutes or until the scones are golden brown. A toothpick inserted in the scones will come out clean when the scones are ready. Remove the pan from the oven and remove the scones from the baking sheet. Cool for 10 minutes before serving.

Bacon, Cheddar and Chive Scones

Makes 8 scones

2 cups all purpose flour
1 tbs. baking powder
1/2 cup cold unsalted butter, cut into small pieces
3/4 cup shredded sharp cheddar cheese
1/4 cup bacon, cooked and crumbled
2 tbs. chopped fresh chives
1/2 tsp. black pepper
1 cup whipping cream

Preheat the oven to 450°. Spray a baking sheet with non stick cooking spray. In a mixing bowl, add the all purpose flour and baking powder. Stir until well combined and add the butter to the dry ingredients. Using a pastry blender, cut the butter into the dry ingredients until you have coarse crumbs. Freeze the dough for 5 minutes.

Add the cheddar cheese, bacon, chives, black pepper and 3/4 cup plus 2 tablespoons whipping cream to the dry ingredients. Stir only until the dough is moistened and combined. Lightly flour your work surface. Pat the dough into a 7" round. The dough will be crumbly. Cut the round into 8 wedges.

Place the scones on the baking sheet. Brush the remaining 2 tablespoons whipping cream over the scones. Bake for 12-15 minutes or until the scones are golden brown. Remove the scones from the oven and serve hot or at room temperature.

Honey Mustard Ham Scones

Makes 16 scones

3 3/4 cups all purpose flour
5 tsp. baking powder
1 tsp. salt
3/4 cup plus 1 tbs. unsalted butter
3 eggs
1/2 cup whole milk
1/3 cup Dijon mustard
1/4 cup honey
1/2 tsp. steak sauce
3/4 cup finely chopped cooked ham

Preheat the oven to 425°. In a mixing bowl, add 3 1/2 cups all purpose flour, baking powder and salt. Stir until combined and add 3/4 cup butter. Using a pastry blender, cut the butter into the dry ingredients until you have coarse crumbs.

In a small bowl, add 2 eggs, milk, Dijon mustard, honey, steak sauce and ham. Whisk until combined and add to the dry ingredients. Stir only until the dough is moistened and combined. Add the remaining 1/4 cup all purpose flour if needed to form a soft dough.

Lightly flour your work surface. Place the dough on your surface and roll into a 12" x 8" rectangle. Cut the dough into eight 4" x 3" rectangles. Cut each rectangle into 2 triangles.

Grease your baking sheet with 1 tablespoon butter. Place the scones on the baking sheet spacing them about 2" apart. In a small bowl, whisk 1 egg until foamy. Brush the egg over the scones. Bake for 10 minutes or until the scones are golden brown. Remove the scones from the oven and serve.

Cheddar Sour Cream Scones

Makes 1 dozen

4 cups all purpose flour
2 tbs. baking powder
1/2 tsp. baking soda
2 tsp. salt
1/4 cup granulated sugar
2 cups shredded cheddar cheese
2 eggs
1 cup sour cream
1/2 cup vegetable oil
1/3 cup whole milk

Preheat the oven to 400°. In a mixing bowl, add the all purpose flour, baking powder, baking soda, salt, granulated sugar and cheddar cheese. Stir until well combined. In a separate bowl, add the eggs, sour cream, vegetable oil and milk. Whisk until well combined and add to the dry ingredients. Mix only until the dough is moistened and combined.

Lightly flour your work surface. Place the dough on your surface and knead 10 times. The dough should be smooth. Pat the dough to 1/2" thickness. Using a 3" round cutter, cut out the scones. Cut the scones as close together as possible on the first cutting. Pat out the dough scraps and cut out the remaining scones.

Spray a baking sheet with non stick cooking spray. Place the scones on the baking sheet about 1" apart. Bake for 15 minutes or until the scones are done and lightly browned. Remove the scones from the oven and serve hot.

Pimento Cheese Scones

Makes 8 scones

2 cups all purpose flour
1 tbs. baking powder
1/2 cup cold unsalted butter, cut into small pieces
3/4 cup shredded sharp cheddar cheese
3 tbs. finely chopped red pimento
1 cup whipping cream

Preheat the oven to 450°. Spray a baking sheet with non stick cooking spray. In a mixing bowl, add the all purpose flour and baking powder. Stir until well combined and add the butter to the dry ingredients. Using a pastry blender, cut the butter into the dry ingredients until you have coarse crumbs. Freeze the dough for 5 minutes.

Add the cheddar cheese, red pimento and 3/4 cup plus 2 tablespoons whipping cream to the dry ingredients. Stir only until the dough is moistened and combined. Lightly flour your work surface. Pat the dough into a 7" round. The dough will be crumbly. Cut the round into 8 wedges.

Place the scones on the baking sheet. Brush the remaining 2 tablespoons whipping cream over the scones. Bake for 12-15 minutes or until the scones are golden brown. Remove the scones from the oven and serve hot or at room temperature.

Ham and Swiss Scones with Mustard Butter

Makes 8 scones

2 cups all purpose flour
1 tbs. baking powder
1/2 cup cold unsalted butter, cut into small pieces
3/4 cup shredded Swiss cheese
3/4 cup cooked ham, finely chopped
2 tbs. chopped fresh chives
1/2 tsp. black pepper
1 cup whipping cream
1/2 cup unsalted butter, softened
1 tbs. spicy brown mustard
1 tbs. minced onion

In a small bowl, add 1/2 cup softened unsalted butter, brown mustard and onion. Stir until combined. Set the butter aside while you make the scones.

Preheat the oven to 450°. Spray a baking sheet with non stick cooking spray. In a mixing bowl, add the all purpose flour and baking powder. Stir until well combined and add 1/2 cup cold butter to the dry ingredients. Using a pastry blender, cut the butter into the dry ingredients until you have coarse crumbs. Freeze the dough for 5 minutes.

Add the Swiss cheese, ham, chives, black pepper and 3/4 cup plus 2 tablespoons whipping cream to the dry ingredients. Stir only until the dough is moistened and combined. Lightly flour your work surface. Pat the dough into a 7" round. The dough will be crumbly. Cut the round into 8 wedges.

Place the scones on the baking sheet. Brush the remaining 2 tablespoons whipping cream over the scones. Bake for 12-15 minutes or until the scones are golden brown. Remove the scones from the oven and serve hot with the mustard butter.

Basic Biscuit Scones

Add any cheese or herb to the batter if desired. Makes 8 scones.

2 cups all purpose flour
2 tsp. baking powder
1/4 tsp. baking soda
1/2 tsp. salt
3 tbs. granulated sugar
1/3 cup unsalted butter, cut into small pieces
1/2 cup plus 1 tbs. whole milk
1 egg, beaten

Preheat the oven to 425°. In a mixing bowl, add the all purpose flour, baking powder, baking soda, salt and 2 tablespoons granulated sugar. Stir until combined and add the butter. Using a pastry blender, cut the butter into the dry ingredients until you have coarse crumbs. Add 1/2 cup milk and the egg to the dry ingredients. Stir only until the dough is moistened and combined.

Lightly flour your work surface. Place the dough on your surface and knead 6 times. The dough should be smooth. Pat the dough into an 8" circle. Lightly spray a baking sheet with non stick cooking spray. Place the circle on the baking sheet. Brush 1 tablespoon milk over the dough and sprinkle 1 tablespoon granulated sugar over the top of the dough.

Bake for 15 minutes or until the scones are golden brown. Remove the pan from the oven and cut the scones into 8 wedges. Serve the scones hot.

3 SWEET BISCUITS

Sweet biscuits are mainly served at brunch or holiday breakfast in the south. I like to make them on the weekend and serve with scrambled eggs, bacon and sausage for a lazy day breakfast.

Sweet biscuits do not rise high like savory biscuits. The addition of sugars to the recipe tends to reduce the rising of the biscuits. They will still rise but do not expect mile high biscuits on all recipes.

Orange Biscuits

Makes 12 biscuits

1 cup plus 2 tbs. all purpose flour
2 tbs. baking powder
1/4 tsp. baking soda
1 tbs. granulated sugar
3 tbs. unsalted butter, chilled
1 egg, beaten
1/3 cup cottage cheese
1 tbs. grated orange zest
3 tbs. orange marmalade
1 tbs. vegetable shortening

Preheat the oven to 400°. Grease your baking sheet with the vegetable shortening. In a mixing bowl, add the all purpose flour, baking powder, granulated sugar, baking soda and butter. Using a pastry blender, cut the butter into the dry ingredients until you have coarse crumbs.

In a small bowl, add the egg, cottage cheese, orange zest and orange marmalade. Stir until well combined and add to the dry ingredients. Stir only until the dough is moistened and combined.

Drop the dough by tablespoonfuls onto your baking sheet. Bake for 13-15 minutes or until the biscuits are done and golden brown. Remove the biscuits from the oven and serve.

Caramel Dessert Biscuits

Makes 8 servings

2 1/4 cups granulated sugar
3 cups boiling water
1/2 cup unsalted butter
1 tsp. vanilla extract
1/4 tsp. salt
2 3/4 cups Bisquick
2/3 cup whole milk

In a large dutch oven over low heat, add 1 cup granulated sugar. Stir constantly and cook until the sugar melts and turns a golden brown. The sugar will clump at first but keep stirring and it will smooth out. Slowly add the boiling water and continue stirring until the sugar dissolves and the caramel is smooth.

Add 1 cup granulated sugar, butter, vanilla extract and salt to the pan. Stir constantly and cook until the mixture resembles a thin syrup. Bring the syrup to a boil and boil for 2 minutes. Remove the pan from the heat and pour the caramel into a 9 x 13 baking pan. Do not use a glass baking pan. The temperature difference may cause the glass to break.

In a mixing bowl, add the Bisquick, milk and 1/4 cup granulated sugar. Stir until the dough is moistened and combined. Lightly flour your work surface and knead the dough 4 times. The dough should be smooth and combined. Do not over work the dough or the biscuits will be tough. Roll the dough out to 1/2" thickness. Using a 2 1/2" biscuit cutter, cut out the biscuits. Cut the biscuits as close together as possible to get as many biscuits as possible on the first cutting. Roll the dough scraps again and cut out the remaining biscuits. Place the biscuits over the caramel in the baking pan.

Preheat the oven to 350°. Bake for 20-25 minutes or until the biscuits are golden brown. Remove the pan from the oven. Immediately place the biscuits on a platter and spoon the caramel sauce over the biscuits. They are delicious with ice cream.

Marmalade Biscuits

Makes about 16 biscuits

2 cups all purpose flour
1 tbs. plus 1 tsp. baking powder
1/2 tsp. salt
1/4 cup plus 1 tbs. vegetable shortening
1 egg, beaten
1/3 cup whole milk
1/3 cup orange marmalade

Preheat the oven to 425°. In a mixing bowl, add the all purpose flour, baking powder and salt. Stir until combined and add the vegetable shortening. Using a pastry blender, cut the shortening into the dry ingredients until you have coarse crumbs.

In a small bowl, whisk together the egg, milk and orange marmalade. Add to the dry ingredients and mix only until a soft dough forms. Lightly flour your work surface. Place the dough on your surface and lightly knead the dough 10 times. Roll the dough to 1/2" thickness. Using a 2" biscuit cutter, cut out the biscuits. Cut the biscuits as close together as possible to cut out as many biscuits as possible on the first cutting. Roll the dough scraps out again and cut out the remaining biscuits.

Place the biscuits on an ungreased baking sheet. Bake for 10 minutes or until the biscuits are done and golden brown. Remove the biscuits from the oven and serve hot.

Simple Sugar Drop Biscuits

Makes 12 biscuits. These biscuits are great by themselves or served with jam or syrup.

2 cups Bisquick
1/2 cup granulated sugar
1/2 tsp. ground cinnamon
1/4 cup unsalted butter
1/2 cup whole milk

Preheat the oven to 425°. In a mixing bowl, add the Bisquick, granulated sugar and cinnamon. Stir until well combined and add the butter. Using a pastry blender, cut the butter into the dry ingredients until you have coarse crumbs. Add the milk and stir until a soft dough forms.

Lightly spray a baking sheet with non stick cooking spray. Drop the dough by heaping tablespoonfuls onto the baking sheet. Bake for 15 minutes or until the biscuits are golden brown. Remove the biscuits from the oven and serve hot.

Easy Lemon Drop Biscuits

Makes about 20 biscuits

3 1/2 cups Bisquick
1/4 cup lemonade drink mix
1/2 cup currants
2 tsp. grated lemon zest
1 2/3 cups whole milk
1 1/2 cups powdered sugar
2 tbs. fresh lemon juice

In a mixing bowl, add the Bisquick, lemonade drink mix, currants, lemon zest and milk. Stir only until the batter is combined and moistened.

Spray your baking sheet with non stick cooking spray. Preheat the oven to 425°. Drop the biscuits by rounded tablespoonfuls onto the baking sheet. Space the biscuits about 2" apart. Wet your fingers and gently shape the biscuits into rounds if desired. Bake for 10 minutes or until the biscuits are done and golden brown.

While the biscuits are baking, make the glaze. In a small bowl, add the powdered sugar and lemon juice. Stir until combined. Drizzle the glaze over the biscuits while still hot. Serve immediately.

Raspberry Almond Biscuits

Makes about 18 biscuits

3 cups all purpose flour
1 tbs. baking powder
1/2 tsp. baking soda
1/8 tsp. salt
1/2 cup granulated sugar
3/4 cup chilled unsalted butter
1 cup fresh raspberries
1/2 cup chopped almonds
1 1/2 tsp. grated orange zest
3/4 cup whole milk
3/4 cup plain yogurt
1 tbs. vegetable shortening

In a mixing bowl, add the all purpose flour, baking powder, baking soda, salt and granulated sugar. Stir until well combined. Cut the butter into small pieces and add to the dry ingredients. Using a pastry blender, cut the butter into the dry ingredients until you have coarse crumbs. Preheat the oven to 400°. Grease your baking sheet with the vegetable shortening.

Add the raspberries and almonds to the bowl. Toss only until the raspberries and almonds are coated with the flour. Stir in the orange zest, milk and yogurt. Mix only until the dough is moistened and combined. The dough will be sticky.

Lightly flour your work surface. Place the dough on the work surface. Toss the dough with the flour on the work surface. The dough should be lightly coated with the flour. With the palm of your hand, slightly flatten the dough. Fold the dough over and slightly flatten the dough again. Turn the dough about 1/4 turn and fold the dough over again. Repeat two more times. The dough should be smooth and soft.

Pat the dough to a 3/4" thickness with your hands. Using a 2 1/2" biscuit cutter, cut out the biscuits. Lightly pat out the dough scraps again to cut out the remaining biscuits. Place the biscuits on your baking sheet. Bake for 20-25 minutes or until the biscuits are done and lightly browned. Remove the biscuits from the oven and serve.

Blueberry Buttermilk Biscuits

Makes about 12 biscuits

2 cups all purpose flour
1 tbs. baking powder
1/4 tsp. baking soda
1 tsp. salt
1/2 cup plus 3 tbs. granulated sugar
1 tsp. grated orange zest
1/3 cup cold vegetable shortening
1 egg, beaten
3/4 cup buttermilk
1/2 cup fresh blueberries
3 tbs. melted unsalted butter
1/4 tsp. ground cinnamon
1/8 tsp. ground nutmeg
1 tbs. vegetable shortening

Preheat the oven to 400°. Grease your baking sheet with 1 tablespoon vegetable shortening. In a mixing bowl, add the all purpose flour, baking powder, 1/2 cup granulated sugar, baking soda, salt, orange zest and 1/3 cup vegetable shortening. Using a pastry blender, cut the shortening into the dry ingredients until you have coarse crumbs.

In a small bowl, add the egg, 1 tablespoon melted butter and buttermilk. Whisk until combined. Add to the dry ingredients and stir only until the dough is moistened and combined. Gently fold in the blueberries, cinnamon and nutmeg.

Lightly flour your work surface. Place the dough on the work surface. With the palm of your hand, slightly flatten the dough. Fold the dough over and slightly flatten the dough again. Turn the dough about 1/4 turn and fold the dough over again. Repeat two more times. The dough should be smooth and soft.

Pat the dough to a 1/2" thickness with your hands. Using a 2 1/2" biscuit cutter, cut out the biscuits. Lightly pat out the dough scraps again to cut out the remaining biscuits. Place the biscuits on your baking sheet. Brush the biscuits with 2 tablespoons melted butter. Sprinkle 2 tablespoons granulated sugar over the biscuits. Bake for 15 minutes or until the biscuits are done and golden brown. Remove the biscuits from the oven and serve.

Lemon Burst Biscuits

Makes about 10 biscuits

2 cups all purpose flour
1 tbs. granulated sugar
2 tsp. baking powder
2 1/2 tsp. finely shredded lemon peel
1/4 tsp. baking soda
1/4 tsp. salt
1/3 cup vegetable shortening
1/3 cup buttermilk
1/3 cup mayonnaise
1 cup powdered sugar
1 tbs. whole milk
1/4 tsp. vanilla extract

Preheat the oven to 450°. In a large mixing bowl, add the all purpose flour, granulated sugar, baking powder, 2 teaspoon lemon peel, baking soda and the salt. Stir until combined and add the vegetable shortening. Using a pastry blender, cut the vegetable shortening into the dry ingredients until you have coarse crumbs. You should have coarse crumbs and still see tiny bits of the shortening when it is ready.

In a small bowl, add the buttermilk and the mayonnaise. Whisk until combined and add to the dry ingredients. Use a fork and stir for a couple of minutes. The dough should begin to form into a ball.

Sprinkle your work surface with additional all purpose flour. Turn the dough onto the work surface. Fold the dough in half and then in half again, rotating the dough slightly each time you fold. Repeat this process three or four times to form layers. Pat the dough to 1/2" thickness. Using a 2" biscuit cutter, cut the biscuits from the dough. Pat the dough scraps out and cut out the remaining biscuits. Place the biscuits on an ungreased baking pan.

Bake for 11-13 minutes or until the biscuits are golden brown. Let the biscuits cool for a few minutes while you make the glaze.

To make the glaze, combine the powdered sugar, 1/2 teaspoon lemon peel, vanilla extract and 1 tablespoon milk. Stir until you have a glaze that will drizzle. Add an additional 1 teaspoon milk if needed to thin the glaze. Drizzle the glaze over the hot biscuits.

Note: Unglazed biscuits will keep for 3 months in the freezer. To reheat the biscuits from the freezer, wrap each biscuit in aluminum foil and bake at 300° for 20 minutes or until the biscuit is hot.

Cranberry Orange Biscuits

Makes 10 biscuits

2 cups all purpose flour
1 tbs. granulated sugar
1 tbs. baking powder
1 tsp. finely shredded orange peel
1/4 tsp. salt
1/4 tsp. baking soda
1/2 cup vegetable shortening
1/2 cup dried cranberries, finely chopped
8 oz. container orange or vanilla yogurt

Preheat the oven to 450°. In a mixing bowl, add the all purpose flour, granulated sugar, baking powder, orange peel, salt and baking soda. Stir until well combined and add the vegetable shortening. Using a pastry blender, cut the shortening into the dry ingredients until you have coarse crumbs.

Add the yogurt and the cranberries to the bowl. Stir with a fork until the dough forms into a ball. This will take about 2 minutes.

Lightly sprinkle your work surface with flour. Fold the dough in half and then in half again, rotating the dough slightly each time you fold. Repeat this process three or four times to form layers. Pat the dough to 1/2" thickness. Using a 2" biscuit cutter, cut the biscuits from the dough. Place the biscuits on an ungreased baking pan. Roll the dough scraps again and cut out the remaining biscuits.

Bake for 10-12 minutes or until the biscuits are golden brown. Serve with hot butter and maple syrup.

Jelly Drop Biscuits

Makes 1 dozen

2 cups all purpose flour
4 tsp. baking powder
2 tsp. granulated sugar
1/2 tsp. salt
1/2 tsp. cream of tartar
1/2 cup vegetable shortening
3/4 cup whole milk
1/3 cup jelly (use your favorite flavor)

Preheat the oven to 450°. In a mixing bowl, add the all purpose flour, granulated sugar, baking powder, salt and cream of tartar. Stir until well mixed and add the vegetable shortening. Using a pastry blender, cut the shortening into the dry ingredients until you have coarse crumbs. You should still be able to see tiny pieces of shortening when finished. Add the milk to the dry ingredients. Stir with a fork until the dough is moistened and combined.

Spray a baking sheet with non stick cooking spray. Drop the dough by tablespoonfuls onto the baking sheet. Space the biscuits about 2" apart. With floured fingers, pat the dough into a biscuit shape. With the back of a small spoon, make an indentation in the top of each biscuit. Spoon 1 teaspoon jelly in the indentation.

Bake for 10-12 minutes or until the biscuits are golden brown. Remove the biscuits from the oven and serve hot. Be careful as the jelly will be very hot.

Nutty Tea Biscuits

Makes about 16 biscuits

2 cups all purpose flour
1 tbs. plus 1 tsp. baking powder
1/2 tsp. salt
1/4 cup granulated sugar
1/4 cup cold vegetable shortening
1/2 cup chopped pecans
1 egg, beaten
1/3 to 1/2 cup whole milk
1 tbs. vegetable shortening

Preheat the oven to 400°. Grease your baking sheet with 1 tablespoon shortening. In a mixing bowl, add the all purpose flour, baking powder granulated sugar, salt and 1/4 cup vegetable shortening. Using a pastry blender, cut the shortening into the dry ingredients until you have coarse crumbs. Stir in the chopped pecans.

In a small bowl, add the egg and 1/3 cup milk. Whisk until well combined. Add to the dry ingredients and stir only until the dough is moistened and combined. Add the remaining milk if needed to make a smooth and moist dough.

Lightly flour your work surface. Place the dough on the work surface. With the palm of your hand, slightly flatten the dough. Fold the dough over and slightly flatten the dough again. Turn the dough about 1/4 turn and fold the dough over again. Repeat two more times. The dough should be smooth and soft.

Pat the dough to a 1/2" thickness with your hands. Using a 2" biscuit cutter, cut out the biscuits. Lightly pat out the dough again to cut out the remaining biscuits. Place the biscuits on your baking sheet. Bake for 15 minutes or until the biscuits are done and golden brown. Remove the biscuits from the oven and serve.

Apple Cinnamon Biscuits

Makes 12 biscuits

2 1/4 cups all purpose flour
1/3 cup granulated sugar
1 tbs. baking powder
1/2 tsp. salt
1/4 tsp. ground nutmeg
1 1/2 tsp. ground cinnamon
6 tbs. cold unsalted butter
3/4 cup whole milk
1 1/2 tsp. vanilla extract
1 1/2 cups finely chopped apples
1 1/2 cups powdered sugar
3 tbs. unsalted butter, softened
2 -3 tbs. hot water

Preheat the oven to 425°. Grease a baking sheet with 1 tablespoon cold butter. In a mixing bowl, add the all purpose flour, granulated sugar, baking powder, salt, ground nutmeg, cinnamon and 5 tablespoons cold butter. Using your fingers, work the butter into the dry ingredients. You should have coarse crumbs when done and still be able to see tiny pieces of the butter.

Add the whole milk, 1 teaspoon vanilla extract and the apples. Stir only until a dough forms. Depending upon the juiciness of your apples, you might have to add a tablespoon or two additional milk or all purpose flour. If the dough is too wet, add all purpose flour. If the dough is too dry, add milk. You need a soft dough that will be slightly sticky but it should not be gooey or runny.

Lightly flour your work surface. Place the dough on the work surface. Fold the dough in half and then in half again, rotating the dough slightly each time you fold. Repeat this process three or four times to form layers. Pat the dough to 3/4" thick. Cut the biscuits out with a 2" biscuit cutter. Roll the dough scraps and cut out the remaining biscuits.

Place the biscuits on the prepared pan. Bake for 12-15 minutes or until the biscuits are done and golden brown. Remove the biscuits from the oven and let them cool for a few minutes while you prepare the glaze.

In a small bowl, add the powdered sugar, 1/2 teaspoon vanilla extract, 3 tablespoons softened butter and 2 tablespoons hot water. Beat with a whisk until you have a glaze. The glaze needs to be pourable. If the glaze is too thick, add another tablespoon hot water. If the glaze is too thin, add a tablespoon or two additional powdered sugar. Pour the glaze over the warm biscuits and serve.

Blueberry Biscuits

Makes 15 biscuits

These biscuits are absolutely delicious. My mother made them often and we gobbled them up in no time. Serve these biscuits with ham, sausage, bacon, yogurt and orange juice for a delicious breakfast.

2 1/4 cups all purpose flour
1/2 cup plus 3 tbs. granulated sugar
1 tbs. baking powder
1 tsp. grated lemon peel
3/4 tsp. salt
1/4 tsp. baking soda
1/3 cup vegetable shortening
1 egg, beaten
3/4 -1 cup whole milk
3/4 cup frozen blueberries (do not thaw)
4 tbs. melted unsalted butter
1/4 tsp. ground cinnamon

Preheat the oven to 400°. Brush 1 tablespoon melted butter onto a baking pan. In a mixing bowl, add the all purpose flour, 1/2 cup granulated sugar, baking powder, lemon peel, salt, baking soda and vegetable shortening. Using a pastry blender, cut the shortening into the dry ingredients until you have coarse crumbs.

In a small bowl, add the egg and 3/4 cup milk. Whisk until combined. Pour the egg and milk into the flour mixture. Stir with a spoon for a minute or two until the dough forms. Add the remaining milk if needed to make a soft dough. Add the frozen blueberries and stir only enough to blend the blueberries. The dough should be soft and slightly sticky.

Lightly sprinkle your work surface with flour. Lightly knead the dough 4 times. The dough should be smooth. Pat the dough to 1/2" thickness. Using a 2" biscuit cutter, cut out the biscuits and place them on the baking pan. Roll the dough scraps and cut out the remaining biscuits. Bake for 12-15 minutes or until the biscuits are done and golden brown.

Make the glaze for the biscuits while they are baking. In a small bowl, add 3 tablespoon melted butter, 3 tablespoon granulated sugar and the cinnamon. Stir until well combined. Brush the glaze across the biscuits when they are hot from the oven. Serve the biscuits hot.

Cinnamon Biscuits

Makes 8 biscuits

2 cups all purpose flour
1 tsp. baking powder
1 tsp. baking soda
1/2 tsp. salt
1/4 cup plus 1 tbs. granulated sugar
2 tsp. ground cinnamon
1/2 cup unsalted butter
3/4 cup whole milk
1/2 cup sliced blanched almonds

Preheat the oven to 400°. In a mixing bowl, add the all purpose flour, baking powder, baking soda, salt, 1/4 cup granulated sugar and 1 teaspoon cinnamon. Stir until combined and add the butter. Using a pastry blender, cut the butter into the dry ingredients until you have coarse crumbs. Add the milk to the bowl and stir only until the dough is moistened and combined.

Lightly flour your work surface. Place the dough on your surface and knead 2 times. The dough should be smooth. Pat the dough to a 3/4" thickness. Using a 2 1/2" biscuit cutter, cut out the biscuits. Cut the biscuits as close together as possible to cut as many biscuits as possible on the first cutting. Roll the dough scraps out again and cut out the remaining biscuits.

Lightly spray a baking sheet with non stick cooking spray. Place the biscuits on the baking sheet. Sprinkle 1 teaspoon cinnamon and the almonds over the biscuits. Sprinkle 1 tablespoon granulated sugar over the top of the biscuits.

Bake for 15-18 minutes or until the biscuits are golden brown. Remove the pan from the oven and serve the biscuits hot.

Up and Down Biscuits

Makes 10 biscuits

2 cups all purpose flour
1 tbs. plus 1 tsp. baking powder
1/2 tsp. salt
1/4 cup plus 3 tsp. granulated sugar
1/2 tsp. cream of tartar
1/2 cup vegetable shortening
2/3 cup whole milk
2 tbs. unsalted butter, melted
1 tbs. ground cinnamon
1 1/2 tbs. vegetable oil

Preheat the oven to 425°. Grease your muffin tin with the vegetable oil. In a mixing bowl, add the all purpose flour, baking powder, salt, 3 teaspoons granulated sugar and cream of tartar. Stir until well combined. Add the vegetable shortening to the bowl. Using a pastry blender, cut the shortening into the dry ingredients until you have coarse crumbs. Add the milk to the dry ingredients and stir until a soft dough forms. The dough will begin to leave the side of the bowl when ready.

Lightly flour your work surface. Place the dough on your surface and knead 5 times. Roll the dough to a 20" x 10" rectangle. Brush the melted butter over the dough. In a small bowl, stir together 1/4 cup granulated sugar and cinnamon. Sprinkle the cinnamon sugar over the dough.

Cut the dough lengthwise into five 2" wide strips. Place the strips, cinnamon side up, on top of each other. Cut the stack into 2" sections. Place each section, cut side down, into the muffin cups.

Bake for 12 minutes or until the biscuits are lightly browned. Remove the biscuits from the oven and immediately remove the biscuits from the pan. Serve the biscuits hot.

Glazed Raisin Biscuits

Makes about 16 biscuits

2 1/2 cups Bisquick
2 tbs. granulated sugar
1 tsp. ground cinnamon
1/2 cup raisins
1 egg, beaten
2/3 cup whole milk
2/3 cup powdered sugar
1 tbs. water
1/4 tsp. vanilla extract

Preheat the oven to 350°. In a mixing bowl, add the Bisquick, granulated sugar, cinnamon and raisins. Stir until well combined. In a small bowl, stir together the egg and milk. Add to the dry ingredients and mix until the dough is combined and moistened.

Lightly flour your work surface. Place the dough on your surface and knead the dough 5 times. Roll the dough to 1/2" thickness. Using a 2" biscuit cutter, cut out the biscuits. Cut the biscuits as close together as possible to cut out as many biscuits as you can on the first cutting. Roll the dough scraps again and cut out the remaining biscuits.

Lightly spray a baking sheet with non stick cooking spray. Place the biscuits on the baking sheets. Bake for 15 minutes or until the biscuits are golden brown. Remove the biscuits from the oven and drizzle the glaze over the hot biscuits.

To make the glaze, add the powdered sugar, water and vanilla extract to a small bowl. Whisk until well combined and drizzle over the hot biscuits.

Pecan Biscuit Twists

Makes 15 servings

2 cups all purpose flour
2 tbs. granulated sugar
1 tbs. baking powder
1/4 tsp. salt
1/2 cup unsalted butter
1 egg
1/2 cup whole milk
1 tbs. unsalted butter, melted
1/4 cup finely chopped pecans
3 tbs. light brown sugar

In a mixing bowl, add the all purpose flour, granulated sugar, baking powder and salt. Stir until well combined. Add 1/2 cup butter to the dry ingredients. Using a pastry blender, cut the butter into the dry ingredients until you have coarse crumbs.

In a small bowl, whisk together the egg and milk. Add to the dry ingredients and stir until the dough is moistened and combined. Lightly flour your work surface. Place the dough on your surface and gently knead the dough 15 times. Roll the dough to a 15" x 8" rectangle. Brush 1 tablespoon melted butter over the dough. Sprinkle the brown sugar and pecans over the dough. Fold the dough in half lengthwise. Using a pizza cutter or sharp knife, cut the dough into 1" strips. Holding a strip at each end, twist the strips twice.

Preheat the oven to 400°. Lightly spray a baking sheet with non stick cooking spray. Place the twists on the baking sheet spacing them about 1" apart. Press the ends down on each strip so they stay twisted on the baking sheet. Bake for 8-10 minutes or until the twists are golden brown. Remove the baking sheet from the oven and cool for a few minutes before serving.

Cinnamon Raisin Biscuits

Makes 1 dozen

1 1/3 cups corn flakes cereal
2 tbs. light brown sugar
1 tsp. ground cinnamon
4 tbs. melted unsalted butter
2 1/2 cups Bisquick
2 tbs. granulated sugar
1/2 cup raisins
1/3 cup whole milk
1/3 cup tonic water
1 1/2 tsp. vanilla extract
1 1/2 cups powdered sugar
2 tbs. sour cream

Preheat the oven to 400°. In a food processor, add the corn flakes, brown sugar and cinnamon. Process until you have fine crumbs. Spoon the mixture into a small bowl and add 2 tablespoons butter. Stir until all the ingredients are moistened.

In a separate mixing bowl, add the Bisquick, granulated sugar, raisins, milk, tonic water and 1/2 teaspoon vanilla extract. Stir only until the dough is moistened and combined. Lightly flour your work surface. Place the dough on your surface and knead 4 times. Sprinkle the corn flake crumb mixture over the dough. Knead only until the crumbs are kneaded in the dough.

Cut the dough into 12 equal pieces. Roll each piece into a ball. Place the balls on the baking sheet spacing them about 1" apart. Lightly press the ball to 1/2" thickness with the palm of your hand. Bake for 15-18 minutes or until the biscuits are golden brown. Remove the biscuits from the oven and cool for a few minutes while you prepare the frosting.

To make the frosting, add 1 teaspoon vanilla extract, 2 tablespoons butter, sour cream and powdered sugar to a mixing bowl. Whisk until well combined and drizzle over the hot biscuits. Serve the biscuits hot.

Orange Marmalade Biscuit Squares

Makes 2 dozen

2 tbs. unsalted butter, softened
1/2 cup orange marmalade
2 cups Bisquick
1/2 cup cold water

Preheat the oven to 425°. Spray an 8" square pan with non stick cooking spray. In a small bowl, add the butter and marmalade. Stir until well combined and spread in the bottom of the pan.

In a mixing bowl, add the Bisquick and water. Stir until well combined and a soft dough forms. Lightly flour your work surface. Place the dough on your surface and knead 5 times. Roll the dough into an 8" square about 1/2" thick. Place the dough on top of the marmalade.

Cut the dough into 24 squares. Bake for 18 minutes or until the biscuit dough is well browned. Remove the pan from the oven and immediately invert the pan onto a serving plate. Serve the biscuits hot.

Apple Cheese Biscuits

Makes 12-14 biscuits

1/3 cup granulated sugar
1/3 cup finely chopped pecans
1/2 tsp. ground cinnamon
1 3/4 cups Bisquick
3/4 cup shredded cheddar cheese
3/4 cup finely chopped apple, peeled
1/3 cup water
1/4 cup unsalted butter, melted

Preheat the oven to 400°. In a small bowl, add the granulated sugar, pecans and cinnamon. Stir until combined. In a separate bowl, add the Bisquick, cheddar cheese and apple. Stir until combined and add the water. Stir only until the dough is combined and begins to form into a ball.

Divide the dough into 18 pieces. Roll each piece into a ball. Place the melted butter in small bowl. Dip each piece in the butter and then roll each piece in the pecan mixture.

Spray a 9" cake pan with non stick cooking spray. Place the pieces, in a single layer, in the cake pan. Bake for 30 minutes or until the biscuits are golden brown. Remove the pan from the oven and cool for 5 minutes before serving.

Coconut Biscuits

Serve fresh fruit and whipped cream over these biscuits for a fabulous dessert. Makes 12 biscuits.

2 cups all purpose flour
3/4 cup sweetened flaked coconut, toasted
2 tbs. granulated sugar
1 tbs. baking powder
1/2 tsp. salt
1/3 cup vegetable shortening
1 cup whole milk
1/2 tsp. vanilla extract
1 tbs. vegetable shortening

Preheat the oven to 450°. Grease your baking sheet with 1 tablespoon vegetable shortening. In a mixing bowl, add the all purpose flour, coconut, granulated sugar, baking powder, salt and 1/3 cup vegetable shortening. Using a pastry blender, cut the shortening into the dry ingredients until you have coarse crumbs.

Add the milk and vanilla extract to the dry ingredients. Stir only until the dough is moistened and combined. Drop 2 tablespoons dough onto the baking sheet for each biscuit. Space the biscuits about 2" apart. Wet your fingers lightly and mold the dough into a biscuit shape. Bake for 10-12 minutes or until the biscuits are done and golden brown. Remove the biscuits from the oven and serve.

Old Fashioned Biscuit Pudding

Makes 8 servings

2 eggs, beaten
2 cups whole milk
1 cup granulated sugar
1 tsp. ground cinnamon
1/4 tsp. ground nutmeg
1/2 tsp. vanilla extract
3 cups crumbled leftover biscuits
1/2 cup raisins, optional

Preheat the oven to 350°. Spray a 9" square pan with non stick cooking spray. In a mixing bowl, add the eggs, milk, granulated sugar, cinnamon, nutmeg and vanilla extract. Whisk until well combined. Add the biscuits and raisins to the bowl. Stir gently until the biscuits are coated in the wet ingredients.

Pour the pudding into the prepared pan. Bake for 40 minutes or until a knife inserted in the center of the pudding comes out clean. Remove the pudding from the oven and cool for 5 minutes before serving.

Chocolate Biscuit Pudding

Makes 6-8 servings

2 dozen small baked biscuits
1/4 cup melted unsalted butter
2 eggs, beaten
2 tbs. unsweetened cocoa
1 1/2 cups granulated sugar
1 to 2 cups milk

Preheat the oven to 350°. Grease a 10" iron skillet with non stick cooking spray or butter. In a mixing bowl, combine the eggs, butter, cocoa and the granulated sugar. Stir until combined. You only need to add enough milk to make the batter a pouring consistency. The amount of milk I need changes every time I make this dish.

Crumble the biscuits into the iron skillet. Pour the batter over the top of the crumbled biscuits. Take a potato masher and mash the biscuits so the batter will absorb into the biscuits. Bake for 50-60 minutes or until the center is set. Remove the skillet from the oven. Serve the pudding warm with whipped cream and chocolate syrup if desired.

4 SWEET SCONES

Sweet scones are my favorite. I love all types of fruit flavors. Try substituting different nuts, fruits, spices and sugar for a unique taste combination.

Brown Sugar Pecan Scones

Makes 8 scones

2 cups all purpose flour
1/2 cup light brown sugar
1 tbs. baking powder
1/2 cup cold unsalted butter, cut into small pieces
1/2 cup chopped pecans
1 cup whipping cream

Preheat the oven to 450°. Spray a baking sheet with non stick cooking spray. In a mixing bowl, add the all purpose flour, brown sugar and baking powder. Stir until well combined and add the butter to the dry ingredients. Using a pastry blender, cut the butter into the dry ingredients until you have coarse crumbs. Freeze the dough for 5 minutes.

Add the pecans and 3/4 cup plus 2 tablespoons whipping cream to the dry ingredients. Stir only until the dough is moistened and combined. Lightly flour your work surface. Pat the dough into a 7" round. The dough will be crumbly. Cut the round into 8 wedges.

Place the scones on the baking sheet. Brush the remaining 2 tablespoons whipping cream over the scones. Bake for 12-15 minutes or until the scones are golden brown. Remove the scones from the oven and serve hot or at room temperature.

Almond Chocolate Chip Scones

Makes 8 servings

3 1/2 cups all purpose flour
5 tsp. baking powder
1/2 cup unsalted butter, chilled
1 cup heavy whipping cream
1 cup semisweet chocolate chips
2 tbs. granulated sugar
1 tsp. salt
4 eggs
1 1/2 tsp. almond extract
1/2 cup slivered almonds, toasted

Preheat the oven to 425°. In a mixing bowl, add the all purpose flour, baking powder, granulated sugar and salt. Add the butter and cut the butter into the dry ingredients using a pastry blender. You should still see tiny pieces of the butter when done.

In a small bowl, add 3 eggs, whipping cream and almond extract. Whisk until well combined and add to the dry ingredients. Mix only until the dough is moistened. Stir in the chocolate chips and almonds.

Lightly flour your work surface. Place the dough on the surface. Knead 6 times or until the dough is smooth. Spray a baking sheet with non stick cooking spray. Place the dough on the baking sheet and form into a 11" circle about 3/4" thick. Cut the dough into 8 wedges and slightly separate the wedges.

Beat the remaining egg in a small bowl. Brush the egg over the wedges. Bake for 12-15 minutes or until the scones are done and golden brown. Remove the scones from the oven and serve warm.

Chocolate Cherry Scones

Makes 8 scones

2 cups all purpose flour
1/2 cup granulated sugar
1 tbs. baking powder
1/2 cup cold unsalted butter, cut into small pieces
1/4 cup dried cherries, chopped
1/4 cup semisweet mini chocolate chips
1 cup whipping cream

Preheat the oven to 450°. Spray a baking sheet with non stick cooking spray. In a mixing bowl, add the all purpose flour, granulated sugar and baking powder. Stir until well combined and add the butter to the dry ingredients. Using a pastry blender, cut the butter into the dry ingredients until you have coarse crumbs. Freeze the dough for 5 minutes.

Add the cherries, chocolate chips and 3/4 cup plus 2 tablespoons whipping cream to the dry ingredients. Stir only until the dough is moistened and combined. Lightly flour your work surface. Pat the dough into a 7" round. The dough will be crumbly. Cut the round into 8 wedges.

Place the scones on the baking sheet. Brush the remaining 2 tablespoons whipping cream over the scones. Bake for 12-15 minutes or until the scones are golden brown. Remove the scones from the oven and serve hot or at room temperature.

Cherry and Cream Scones

Makes 6-8 scones

2 cups all purpose flour
1 tbs. baking powder
1/4 tsp. salt
1/3 cup plus 2 tbs. granulated sugar
1/3 cup unsalted butter
1 1/2 cups whipping cream
3 oz. pkg. dried cherries

Preheat the oven to 375°. In a mixing bowl, add the all purpose flour, baking powder, salt and 1/3 cup granulated sugar. Stir until combined and add the butter. Using a pastry blender, cut the butter into the dry ingredients until you have coarse crumbs. Add 1 1/4 cups whipping cream and cherries to the dry ingredients. Stir only until the dough is moistened and combined.

Lightly flour your work surface. Place the dough on your surface and knead 6 times. The dough should be smooth. Pat the dough to a 1/2" thickness. Using a 5" cutter, cut out the scones. Cut the scones as close together as possible to cut out as many scones as possible on the first cutting. Pat out the remaining dough and cut out the remaining scones. Lightly spray a baking sheet with non stick cooking spray. Place the scones on the baking sheet. Brush 1/4 cup whipping cream over the scones. Sprinkle 2 tablespoons granulated sugar over the top of the dough.

Bake for 12-15 minutes or until the scones are golden brown. Remove the pan from the oven and serve the scones hot.

Cranberry Biscuit Scones

Makes 8 scones

2 cups all purpose flour
2 tsp. baking powder
1/2 tsp. salt
1/4 cup granulated sugar
1/4 tsp. baking soda
1/4 cup fresh chopped cranberries
1/3 cup dried cranberries
1 egg
6 tbs. butter
1/2 cup whole milk
1 egg white, beaten

Preheat the oven to 400°. In a food processor, add the all purpose flour, baking powder, salt, granulated sugar, baking soda, fresh cranberries, dried cranberries, egg and the butter. Process until well mixed. Place the dough in a mixing bowl and add the milk. Stir until you have a soft dough.

Lightly flour your work surface. Turn the dough onto the work surface and roll out to about 3/4" thick. Cut out the scones with a 2" biscuit cutter and place on a ungreased baking sheet. Brush the egg white over the top of the scones. Bake for 10-12 minutes or until lightly browned. Remove the scones from the oven and serve hot.

Lemon Poppy Seed Scones

Makes 8 servings

2 cups all purpose flour
2 tsp. baking powder
1/4 tsp. baking soda
1/2 tsp. salt
2 tbs. granulated sugar
2 tsp. grated lemon zest
1 tsp. poppy seeds
1/3 cup unsalted butter, cut into small pieces
1/2 cup whole milk
1 egg
1 1/2 tbs. fresh lemon juice
1 cup powdered sugar

Preheat the oven to 425°. In a mixing bowl, add the all purpose flour, baking powder, baking soda, salt, granulated sugar, lemon zest and poppy seeds. Stir until combined and add the butter. Using a pastry blender, cut the butter into the dry ingredients until you have coarse crumbs. Add the egg and milk to the dry ingredients. Stir only until the dough is moistened and combined.

Lightly flour your work surface. Place the dough on your surface and knead 6 times. The dough should be smooth. Pat the dough into an 8" circle. Lightly spray a baking sheet with non stick cooking spray. Place the circle on the baking sheet.

Bake for 15 minutes or until the scones are golden brown. Remove the pan from the oven and cut the scones into 8 wedges. Drizzle the lemon glaze over the scones before serving.

To make the lemon glaze, add the lemon juice and powdered sugar to a small bowl. Whisk until well combined and the glaze is smooth.

Apricot Ginger Scones

Makes 8 scones

2 cups all purpose flour
1/2 cup granulated sugar
1 tbs. baking powder
1/2 cup cold unsalted butter, cut into small pieces
1/2 cup dried apricots, chopped
2 tbs. minced crystallized ginger
1 cup whipping cream

Preheat the oven to 450°. Spray a baking sheet with non stick cooking spray. In a mixing bowl, add the all purpose flour, granulated sugar and baking powder. Stir until well combined and add the butter to the dry ingredients. Using a pastry blender, cut the butter into the dry ingredients until you have coarse crumbs. Freeze the dough for 5 minutes.

Add the apricots, ginger and 3/4 cup plus 2 tablespoons whipping cream to the dry ingredients. Stir only until the dough is moistened and combined. Lightly flour your work surface. Pat the dough into a 7" round. The dough will be crumbly. Cut the round into 8 wedges.

Place the scones on the baking sheet. Brush the remaining 2 tablespoons whipping cream over the scones. Bake for 12-15 minutes or until the scones are golden brown. Remove the scones from the oven and serve hot or at room temperature.

Oatmeal Raisin Scones

Makes 12 scones

1 cup all purpose flour
3 tbs. light brown sugar
1 1/2 tsp. baking powder
1/2 tsp. ground cinnamon
1/3 cup unsalted butter
1 cup quick oats
1/2 cup raisins, chopped
1 egg
1/4 cup plus 2 tbs. whole milk

Preheat the oven to 400°. Spray a baking sheet with non stick cooking spray. In a mixing bowl, add the all purpose flour, brown sugar, cinnamon and baking powder. Stir until well combined and add the butter to the dry ingredients. Using a pastry blender, cut the butter into the dry ingredients until you have coarse crumbs. Add the oats and raisins to the dry ingredients. Stir until combined.

In a small bowl, add the egg and 1/4 cup milk. Whisk until combined and add to the dry ingredients. Stir only until the dough is moistened and combined. The dough will be slightly sticky. Lightly flour your work surface. Pat the dough into a 7" round. Cut the round into 12 wedges.

Place the scones on the baking sheet. Brush the remaining 2 tablespoons milk over the scones. Bake for 10-13 minutes or until the scones are lightly brown. Remove the scones from the oven and serve hot or at room temperature.

Mocha Pecan Scones

Makes 8 scones

2 cups all purpose flour
2 tsp. baking powder
1/4 tsp. baking soda
1/2 tsp. salt
1/4 cup plus 1 tbs. granulated sugar
1/3 cup unsalted butter, cut into small pieces
1 egg, beaten
1/2 cup plus 1 tbs. whole milk
1 tsp. instant espresso powder
1/2 cup chopped pecans
3/4 cup semisweet chocolate chips

Preheat the oven to 425°. In a mixing bowl, add the all purpose flour, baking powder, baking soda, salt and 1/4 cup granulated sugar. Stir until combined and add the butter. Using a pastry blender, cut the butter into the dry ingredients until you have coarse crumbs. Add the egg, 1/2 cup milk and espresso powder to a separate mixing bowl. Whisk until the espresso powder dissolves and add to the dry ingredients. Add the pecans and 1/2 cup chocolate chips to the dry ingredients. Stir only until the dough is moistened and combined.

Lightly flour your work surface. Place the dough on your surface and knead 6 times. The dough should be smooth. Divide the dough into two equal portions. Pat each portion into a 6" circle. Cut each circle into 4 wedges.

Lightly spray a baking sheet with non stick cooking spray. Place the scones on the baking sheet about 1" apart. Brush 1 tablespoon milk over the dough and sprinkle 1 tablespoon granulated sugar over the top of the dough.

Bake for 15 minutes or until the scones are golden brown. Remove the pan from the oven. In a small bowl, add 1/4 cup chocolate chips. Microwave for 15 seconds or until the chips are warm. Stir until the chocolate chips melt. Drizzle the melted chocolate over the scones before serving.

Gingerbread Scones

Makes 8 scones

2 cups all purpose flour
3 tbs. light brown sugar
2 tsp. baking powder
1 tsp. ground ginger
1/2 tsp. baking soda
1/2 tsp. ground cinnamon
1/8 tsp. salt
1/4 cup unsalted butter
1 egg yolk, beaten
1/3 cup molasses
1/4 cup whole milk
1 egg white, beaten

Preheat the oven to 400°. In a large mixing bowl, add the all purpose flour, light brown sugar, baking powder, ginger, baking soda, cinnamon and the salt. Stir until well combined.

Add the butter to the dry ingredients. Using a pastry blender, cut the butter into the dry ingredients until you have coarse crumbs. In a small bowl, add the egg yolk, molasses and the milk. Stir until well combined. Pour the milk mixture into the bowl with the dry ingredients. Stir for a couple minutes or until the dough is moistened and combined.

Sprinkle your work surface with all purpose flour. Place the dough on the surface and knead 5-6 times or until the dough is almost smooth. Pat the dough with your hands into an 8" circle. Cut the dough into 8 slices similar to pie slices.

Place the scones on an ungreased baking sheet. Brush the egg white across the top and sides of the scone. Bake for 12-18 minutes or until the bottom of the scones are brown. Serve with butter if desired.

Orange Pecan Scones

Makes 16 scones

1/3 cup unsalted butter
2 cups self rising flour
3/4 cup whole milk
3 tbs. granulated sugar
1 tsp. grated orange zest
1 tsp. vanilla extract
1/2 cup chopped pecans
2 tbs. melted unsalted butter

Preheat the oven to 425°. Spray a baking sheet with non stick cooking spray. In a mixing bowl, add the self rising flour and 1/3 cup butter. Using a pastry blender, cut the butter into the flour until you have coarse crumbs. Add the milk, granulated sugar, orange zest, vanilla extract and pecans. Stir until the dough is moistened and combined. You should have a soft dough.

Lightly flour your work surface. Place the dough on your surface and lightly knead the dough 4 times. Divide the dough into two equal portions. Shape each portion into a 7" circle. Place the circles on your baking sheet. Cut each circle into 8 scones. Do not separate the scones.

Bake for 12-15 minutes or until the scones are lightly browned. Remove the scones from the oven and brush 2 tablespoons melted butter over the scones. Serve the scones hot.

Cranberry Pistachio Scones

Makes 8 scones

2 cups all purpose flour
1/2 cup granulated sugar
1 tbs. baking powder
1/2 cup cold unsalted butter, cut into small pieces
1/4 cup dried cranberries, chopped
1/4 cup roasted and salted pistachios, chopped
1 cup whipping cream

Preheat the oven to 450°. Spray a baking sheet with non stick cooking spray. In a mixing bowl, add the all purpose flour, granulated sugar and baking powder. Stir until well combined and add the butter to the dry ingredients. Using a pastry blender, cut the butter into the dry ingredients until you have coarse crumbs. Freeze the dough for 5 minutes.

Add the cranberries, pistachios and 3/4 cup plus 2 tablespoons whipping cream to the dry ingredients. Stir only until the dough is moistened and combined. Lightly flour your work surface. Pat the dough into a 7" round. The dough will be crumbly. Cut the round into 8 wedges.

Place the scones on the baking sheet. Brush the remaining 2 tablespoons whipping cream over the scones. Bake for 12-15 minutes or until the scones are golden brown. Remove the scones from the oven and serve hot or at room temperature.

Cranberry Pumpkin Scones

Makes 8 scones

1 1/4 cups all purpose flour
1/2 cup whole wheat flour
1/4 cup granulated sugar
1 tsp. baking powder
1/2 tsp. baking soda
1/2 tsp. ground cinnamon
1/2 tsp. ground nutmeg
1/4 cup unsalted butter, cut into pieces
1/2 cup canned pumpkin
1/2 cup applesauce
1/3 cup chopped walnuts
1/3 cup dried cranberries
1 tbs. light brown sugar

Preheat the oven to 350°. Grease a baking pan with non stick cooking spray. In a large bowl, add the all purpose flour, whole wheat flour, granulated sugar, baking powder, baking soda, cinnamon, nutmeg and butter. Using a pastry blender, cut the butter into the dry ingredients until you have coarse crumbs.

In a small bowl, add the applesauce, pumpkin, cranberries and walnuts. Stir until well combined and add to the dry ingredients. Stir with a fork only until the dough is moistened and combined.

Sprinkle your work surface with all purpose flour. Place the dough on the surface. Knead the dough about 5-6 times or until the dough forms and is smooth. Pat the dough into an 8" circle. Sprinkle the top of the scones with the brown sugar. Cut the circle into 8 wedges.

Place the scones on the prepared baking sheet. Bake for 25-30 minutes or until the scones are browned. Remove the scones from the oven and serve hot or at room temperature.

Cranberry Orange Scones

Makes 8 servings

2 cups all purpose flour
1 tbs. baking powder
1/2 tsp. baking soda
1/4 tsp. salt
3 tbs. granulated sugar
1 tbs. grated orange zest
1/2 cup unsalted butter, cut into small pieces
2/3 cup plus 1 tbs. whole milk
1 cup dried cranberries

Preheat the oven to 425°. In a mixing bowl, add the all purpose flour, baking powder, baking soda, salt, 2 tablespoons granulated sugar and orange zest. Stir until combined and add the butter. Using a pastry blender, cut the butter into the dry ingredients until you have coarse crumbs. Add the cranberries and 2/3 cup milk to the dry ingredients. Stir only until the dough is moistened and combined.

Lightly flour your work surface. Place the dough on your surface and knead 6 times. The dough should be smooth. Pat the dough into an 8" circle. Lightly spray a baking sheet with non stick cooking spray. Place the circle on the baking sheet. Brush 1 tablespoon milk over the dough and sprinkle 1 tablespoon granulated sugar over the top of the dough.

Bake for 15 minutes or until the scones are golden brown. Remove the pan from the oven and cut the scones into 8 wedges. Serve the scones hot.

Orange Ginger Scones

Makes 1 dozen

2 cups all purpose flour
4 tbs. granulated sugar
2 tsp. baking powder
2 tsp. ground ginger
1/2 tsp. salt
1/4 tsp. baking soda
1/2 cup cold butter, cut into small pieces
1 egg
3/4 cup sour cream
1 1/2 tsp. grated orange zest

Preheat the oven to 400°. In a mixing bowl, add the all purpose flour, baking powder, ginger, salt, baking soda and 2 tablespoons granulated sugar. Stir until combined and add the butter. Using a pastry blender, cut the butter into the dry ingredients until you have coarse crumbs. In a small bowl, add the egg, sour cream and orange zest. Whisk until well combined and add to the dry ingredients. Stir only until the dough is moistened and combined.

Lightly flour your work surface. Place the dough on your surface and knead 6 times. The dough should be smooth. Divide the dough into two portions. Pat each portion into a 7" circle. Cut each circle into 6 wedges.

Lightly spray a baking sheet with non stick cooking spray. Place the scones on the baking sheet. Sprinkle 2 tablespoons granulated sugar over the top of the scones. Bake for 10-12 minutes or until the scones are golden brown. Remove the pan from the oven and serve the scones hot.

Dried Blueberry Scones

Makes 8 scones

1/3 cup plus 2 tbs. granulated sugar
2 cups all purpose flour
1/4 cup nonfat dry milk powder
1/4 tsp. salt
1/3 cup vegetable shortening
1 tsp. dried lemon peel, minced
1 tsp. vanilla extract
1 egg, beaten
1/4 cup water
1 cup dried blueberries
2 tbs. whole milk

Preheat the oven to 400°. In a large mixing bowl, add 1/3 cup granulated sugar, all purpose flour, dry milk powder, salt and vegetable shortening. Using a pastry blender, cut the vegetable shortening into the dry ingredients until you have coarse crumbs. Add the blueberries, lemon peel, vanilla extract, egg and water to the dry ingredients. Stir with a fork and mix until the dough is moistened and combined.

Sprinkle your work surface lightly with all purpose flour. Place the dough on the work surface. Knead the dough 5 times or until the dough is smooth. Pat the dough into an 8" circle. Cut the circle into 8 wedges.

Place the scones on an ungreased baking sheet. Bake for 10-12 minutes or until the scones are lightly browned. Brush the scones with the milk and sprinkle 2 tablespoons granulated sugar over the scones. Remove the scones from the oven and serve hot.

Double Orange Scones

Makes 8 servings

11 oz. can mandarin oranges, drained and chopped
1 cup all purpose flour
1 cup whole wheat flour
2 1/2 tsp. baking powder
1/4 tsp. salt
4 tbs. granulated sugar
2 tsp. grated orange zest
1/3 cup chilled unsalted butter, cut into small pieces
1/3 cup whole milk
1 egg, beaten
1/2 cup unsalted butter, softened
2 tbs. orange marmalade

In a small bowl, stir together 1/2 cup softened butter and orange marmalade. Set the butter aside and serve with the hot scones. Pat the mandarin orange slices with paper towels to remove most of the moisture.

Preheat the oven to 400°. In a mixing bowl, add the all purpose flour, baking powder, whole wheat flour, salt, 3 tablespoons granulated sugar and orange zest. Stir until combined and add 1/3 cup chilled butter. Using a pastry blender, cut the butter into the dry ingredients until you have coarse crumbs. Add the mandarin oranges, egg and milk to the dry ingredients. Stir only until the dough is moistened and combined.

Lightly flour your work surface. Place the dough on your surface and knead 6 times. The dough should be smooth. Pat the dough into an 8" circle. Lightly spray a baking sheet with non stick cooking spray. Place the dough on the baking sheet. Sprinkle 1 tablespoon granulated sugar over the top of the dough.

Bake for 20 minutes or until the scones are golden brown. Remove the pan from the oven and cut the scones into 8 wedges. Serve the scones hot with the orange butter.

Currant Scones

Makes 1 dozen

3 cups all purpose flour
1 tbs. baking powder
2 tbs. granulated sugar
2 tbs. unsalted butter
1/2 cup currants
1 egg
3/4 cup plus 2 tbs. whole milk

Preheat the oven to 450°. In a mixing bowl, add the all purpose flour, baking powder and granulated sugar. Stir until combined and add the butter to the bowl. Using a pastry blender, cut the butter into the dry ingredients until you have coarse crumbs. Add the currants and stir until combined.

In a small bowl, add the egg and 3/4 cup milk. Whisk until combined and add to the dry ingredients. Stir only until a soft moist dough forms. Lightly flour your work surface and place the dough on your surface. Knead the dough 8 times.

Roll the dough to 1/2" thickness. Using a 2" biscuit cutter, cut out the scones. Roll the dough scraps again and cut out the remaining scones. Place the scones on an ungreased baking sheet. Brush 2 tablespoons milk over the scones.

Bake for 10 minutes or until the scones are golden brown. Remove the scones from the oven and serve them hot.

Bacon Date Scones

Makes 16 scones

2 1/4 cups all purpose flour
1/3 cup granulated sugar
4 tsp. baking powder
8 tbs. unsalted butter, chilled
1/2 cup bacon, cooked and crumbled
1/2 cup pitted dates, chopped
1/2 cup chopped pecans
3/4 cup whipping cream
1 egg
1/2 cup orange marmalade

Preheat the oven to 400°. In a mixing bowl, add the all purpose flour, baking powder and granulated sugar. Stir until combined and add 6 tablespoons butter. Using a pastry blender, cut the butter into the dry ingredients until you have coarse crumbs.

In a small bowl, add the bacon, dates and pecans to the bowl. Stir until combined. Add 1 cup bacon mixture to the dry ingredients. In a small bowl, whisk together the egg and whipping cream. Add to the dry ingredients and stir until the dough is moistened and combined. Divide the dough into two equal portions and shape each portion into a ball.

Lightly spray a large baking sheet with non stick cooking spray. Place each portion on the baking sheet. Space the scones about 4" apart. Pat each portion into an 8" circle. Cut each circle into 8 wedges but do not separate the wedges. Sprinkle the remaining bacon mixture over the top of the scones. Bake for 15 minutes or until the scones are lightly browned. Remove the scones from the oven and drizzle the glaze over the hot scones.

To make the glaze, add the orange marmalade and 2 tablespoons butter to a small microwavable bowl. Microwave for 30 seconds or until the butter is melted and the marmalade is hot. Stir until combined and drizzle over the hot scones before serving.

Chapter Index

Savory Biscuits

Savory Scones

Cheddar Cheese Scones, 64
Basil Parmesan Scones, 65
Onion Scones, 66
Pear Asiago Scones, 67
Blue Cheese Nut Scones, 68
Cheddar Herb Scones, 69
Tabasco Parmesan Scones, 70
Bacon, Cheddar and Chive Scones, 71
Honey Mustard Ham Scones, 72
Cheddar Sour Cream Scones, 73
Pimento Cheese Scones, 74
Ham and Swiss Scones with Mustard Butter, 75
Basic Biscuit Scones, 76

Sweet Biscuits

Orange Biscuits, 78
Caramel Dessert Biscuits, 79
Marmalade Biscuits, 80
Simple Sugar Drop Biscuits, 80
Easy Lemon Drop Biscuits, 81
Raspberry Almond Biscuits, 82
Blueberry Buttermilk Biscuits, 83
Lemon Burst Biscuits, 84
Cranberry Orange Biscuits, 85
Jelly Drop Biscuits, 86
Nutty Tea Biscuits, 87
Apple Cinnamon Biscuits, 88
Blueberry Biscuits, 89
Cinnamon Biscuits, 90
Up and Down Biscuits, 91
Glazed Raisin Biscuits, 92
Pecan Biscuit Twists, 93
Cinnamon Raisin Biscuits, 94
Orange Marmalade Biscuit Squares, 95
Apple Cheese Biscuits, 95
Coconut Biscuits, 96
Old Fashioned Biscuit Pudding, 96
Chocolate Biscuit Pudding, 97

Sweet Scones

Brown Sugar Pecan Scones, 99
Almond Chocolate Chip Scones, 100
Chocolate Cherry Scones, 101
Cherry and Cream Scones, 102
Cranberry Biscuit Scones, 103
Lemon Poppy Seed Scones, 104
Apricot Ginger Scones, 105
Oatmeal Raisin Scones, 106
Mocha Pecan Scones, 107
Gingerbread Scones, 108
Orange Pecan Scones, 109
Cranberry Pistachio Scones, 110
Cranberry Pumpkin Scones, 111
Cranberry Orange Scones, 112
Orange Ginger Scones, 113
Dried Blueberry Scones, 114
Double Orange Scones, 115
Currant Scones, 116
Bacon Date Scones, 117

ABOUT THE AUTHOR

Lifelong southerner who lives in Bowling Green, KY. Priorities in life are God, family and pets. I love to cook, garden and feed most any stray animal that walks into my yard. I love old cookbooks and cookie jars. Huge NBA fan who loves to spend hours watching basketball games. Enjoy cooking for family and friends and hosting parties and reunions. Can't wait each year to build gingerbread houses for the kids.